Widening *the* Welcome *of* Your Church

Biblical Hospitality &
The Vital Congregation

New Edition – Study Guide Included

Fred Bernhard and Steve Clapp

**ANDREW
CENTER
RESOURCES**

Widening the Welcome Of Your Church

Biblical Hospitality & The Vital Congregation

Fred Bernhard and Steve Clapp

Drawing by Kimberly J. Haugh

ISBN 0-9637206-9-4

Manufactured in the United States of America

Contents

Rather than a traditional table of contents, we've chosen to include not only the chapter titles but also the core concept which is covered in each chapter.

Hospitality: Not Optional and Not Safe　　　　　　**9**
　　Concept: In a society filled with both rational
　　and irrational fear, God calls us to embrace the
　　stranger, to recognize the presence of Christ in
　　the one who is unknown. Hospitality is not an
　　option for the church, and it is not always safe.

A Biblical Look at Hospitality　　　　　　**19**
　　Concept: The Old and New Testaments both
　　regard hospitality as an obligation. The biblical
　　texts do not question the worthiness of the
　　needy stranger but instead examine the faith-
　　fulness of the one from whom hospitality is needed.

The Oakland Experience　　　　　　**27**
　　Concept: A rural congregation belonging to a
　　denomination which is declining in membership
　　experienced increased vitality and growth as a
　　result of biblical hospitality. The same emphasis
　　can work in any congregation.

What Motivates Us?　　　　　　**35**
　　Concept: The practice of hospitality won't trans-
　　form your congregation if it is viewed as only one
　　more in a series of programs to strengthen the
　　church. The majority of the congregation must,
　　at a fundamental level, come to feel that hospitality
　　is a core part of our responsibility as Christians and
　　come to share a vision of the congregation as a
　　truly welcoming place.

Experiencing Hospitality In the Church   **43**
    Concept: The caring host provides the kind of
    acceptance and the opportunities which respond
    to the needs and comfort level of the guest.

Welcoming Strangers   **55**
    Concept: While our culture teaches us to fear
    strangers, we also know that our best friends
    were once strangers to us. Life is transformed
    when we see the stranger as potential friend.

Welcoming Children   **65**
    Concept: Children belong as fully to the Christian
    community as do their parents. Our Lord always
    showed special consideration to children; and we
    should do the same, which means looking at the
    life of the church from a child's perspective.

Welcoming Teenagers   **81**
    Concept: Teenagers are struggling for identity
    and coping with a multitude of pressures. The
    church's hospitality should offer them a safe
    place to be themselves and to grow in their
    relationships with Christ and other people.

Welcoming Young Adults   **89**
    Concept: Almost all churches want to reach
    more young adults, especially young adult
    families. Making young adults part of the
    church, however, either requires change or
    causes change.

Hospitality and the Overlooked   **103**
    Concept: The congregation which takes
    seriously a biblical understanding of hospi-
    tality does not place restrictions on its
    welcome and actively seeks out those whom
    others might overlook.

How Welcoming are Your Physical Facilities?   **113**
    Concept: The church's physical facilities can be
    part of your congregation's welcome or can be a
    barrier to participation by members and visitors.

The Changing Shape of Worship and Program   **123**
    Concept: We should continually strive to make
    the services and programs of the church expressions
    of the welcome we want extended to all people.

Resources and References   **135**

About The Andrew Center   **141**

---

*At the conclusion of this book, you'll find a
Study Guide, which was originally a separate
publication. That Guide has been included
in this printing as a service to individuals
and congregations.*

This book is dedicated to:

Jesus Christ, from whose invitation I experienced
God's welcome, acceptance, and the affirmation of my
personhood; and who confirmed for me that, by God's
grace, I have been adopted into God's family.

My family:
- spouse, Joice
- daughter, Barbara, and sons, Howard and Tom;
  their spouses, Wayne, Patty, and Melodie
- grandchildren, Kimberly and spouse Cary;
  Lori and spouse Randy; Carrie; Robert; Melissa;
  Rachel; and Michael
- our great grandchildren, David and Jordan

They daily teach me how to live in an hospitable relational
environment as a microcosm of God's family.

The Oakland Congregation, a covenanted body of people,
whose dedication and practice allowed this book to become
a reality. In our journey together, we came to believe that
the welcome and acceptance we experienced in Christ must
be shared with the outsider until all people experience that
same welcome and acceptance – and hear Christ's invitation
to become sons and daughters in God's glorious family.

Fred Bernhard

And to:

The Church Universal, that great company of saints
who belong to the body of Christ and whose reality
transcends denomination, race, nation, culture, time,
and space. That Church which shows hospitality
to all people, in all times, and in all places.

My brothers and sisters in Christ at Lincolnshire Church
who have embraced me from the moment of my arrival
in Fort Wayne and who continue to renew my faith.

Steve Clapp

We both extend our thanks for the contributions made to this book by:
Paul Mundey, Barb Faga, Karen Carlson, Carolyn Egolf, Holly
Carcione, Kristen Leverton, Claire Long, Christine Brewer, Barbara
Menke, Jerry Peterson, and the staff of Evangel Press.

Welcome one another, therefore, just as Christ has welcomed you, for the glory of God.

Romans 15:7

Hospitality:
Not Optional and Not Safe

Concept: In a society filled with both rational and irrational fear, God calls us to embrace the stranger, to recognize the presence of Christ in the one who is unknown. Hospitality is not an option for the church, and it is not always safe.

"Search Continues for Missing Child"

"Violent Crime Index Rises Again"

"New Wave of Break-ins in Pine Valley"

"Vandalism at All-Time High"

"Gun Ownership Continues to Climb"

We've all read and heard the headlines – in newspapers and magazines, on radio and television, and even on Internet services. We don't feel safe as a society, and not all that fear is irrational!

This book, however, grows out of a conviction that the way of Christ is different than the way of the world. We do not want to live foolishly, but we do want to live consistently with what our Lord has taught us. In a society increasingly filled with fear and distrust, people are hungry for the kind of acceptance and intimacy which the church, at its best, offers.

Many of us form our basic attitudes toward the unknown in general and toward strangers in particular during our childhood years. Fred and Steve were both blessed with early experiences which helped them feel comfortable with strangers.

We want our respective contributions to this book, for the most part, to appear seamless, for there to be no abrupt shifts from person to person in narration, and for the identification of whether it is Fred or Steve speaking to be irrelevant. As we begin our account, however, we each want to share childhood stories.

Roots in Childhood

Fred: My family lived on a farm in Pennsylvania along the main thoroughfare between Harrisburg and Lancaster. Hoboes, as we called them, made frequent visits to our farm for hot meals and overnight lodging. I came to understand the aid which my parents gave travelers as a Christian practice and learned to enjoy contact with these strangers. Curiosity led me to explore who they were, why they were transients, and why they chose our farm to request meals and lodging. The memory of those shabbily dressed persons wearily trudging up our farm lane, with knapsacks slung over their stooped shoulders and canes in hand, evokes a pleasant and precious nostalgia.

On Sundays my parents would invite other church families to our home for dinner. I grew up seeing this practice as an integral part of the Sunday worship experience. The people with whom we shared in worship were also our friends.

Likewise, visitors to church were invited home for a sumptuous noon meal and encouraged to spend the afternoon in conversation. Lodging would be offered if the visitor had come from a distance.

Newcomers who moved to our community would also be invited into our home for a meal. While they were with us, we would inquire about their religious affiliation, and depending on their answer, would extend a general or specific invitation to worship with our family if that was appropriate. We would witness to the faith which we held but only at the point of their inquiry; it never occurred to us to attempt to force our belief on others.

If these newcomers had not yet accepted Christ as Lord and Savior, that invitation would certainly be extended to them at the appropriate point – but not apart from the context of regular worship and Bible study. This gradual incorporation allowed newcomers to know who we were and what was expected of them before a commitment was made.

For my family, practicing hospitality was an end in itself. It was an expression to others of our thanks to God for Christ's generosity to us. This faith sharing often led others to a commitment to discipleship, but that was viewed by us as a by-product of our need to respond to them in a loving manner. The hobo, the visitor, and the newcomer received our gifts as the outward expression of our faith.

Part of the reason that my parents were so effective in extending hospitality is that they knew what it meant to be a stranger. Their Brethren beliefs were considered somewhat peculiar and were unpopular in the larger community. The rejection which they had experienced enabled them to better understand the sense of isolation which others could experience.

Steve: My childhood experiences were different than Fred's in terms of geography and denomination. I grew up in down-state Illinois and spent my childhood and teenage years in the Methodist (now United Methodist) Church. My experiences with strangers, however, were remarkably similar to those of Fred.

My father was the township supervisor for the community in which we lived. That meant, among other things, that he was responsible for all the aid and relief which was given to persons who were unemployed or homeless or just passing through town. People for whom the forces of life had been difficult came to our home, seeking help from my father. What they encountered has little in common with how such assistance is given through government agencies today. My father's greeting to them was always warm and personal, and he made it clear that he was glad they had come. He would invite them to join us for a meal, and he taught me to relate to them as to any other guests in our home.

I can remember some of my friends at school being shocked when they occasionally discovered that we had as guests in our home people who were known alcoholics, ex-convicts, and hoboes. Some of their parents talked about the fact that my father and mother didn't seem to use good judgment in differentiating between those who were simply "down on their luck" and those who were "the root of their own problem." I can certainly remember my father urging some to start attending A A meetings, and I cannot even count the number of times he made calls to arrange temporary housing and to open the door for employment. But I do not remember his ever barring anyone from our dinner table or sending out into the night anyone who did not have a place to stay. I remember his treating everyone with considerable graciousness and kindness, and I remember the transforming effect which that had on many lives.

My parents likewise extended a warm welcome to persons who visited our church and to persons who were new in the community. In part because the town was small enough for "everyone to know everyone" (or at least to think that they did!), local residents were pulled between enormous curiosity and an almost irrational distrust of those who were newly arrived. My parents, however, had both moved there from other places and knew what it was like to come as a stranger.

Both my parents had been raised in the church, and the Bible was extremely important in their lives. One of my father's favorite passages of Scripture was Matthew 25:31-46 about encountering Christ "in the least of these."

Living in Fear

We have all experienced rejection because we were strangers to others. We know what it feels like to be ordered to present a driver's license and a credit card to get a check accepted at a store. We know the fear of having car trouble on the highway and not having anyone stop. We know the anxiety of trying to find our way around an unfamiliar neighborhood or city.

In many respects, fear and distrust seem to have spread like a cancer in our land. Symbols of openness are disappearing from the North American scene as we barricade ourselves from strangers in an effort to protect ourselves and our possessions. Electric door locks on cars, double locks on house doors, security alarms, guard dogs, lobby guards, security officers, increased numbers of police, and the military are just a few signs of our deep-seated fear of the stranger. We hide our money, lock our doors, chain our bikes, and look over our shoulders.

News reports of break-ins, break-outs, and blackouts feed our fears. We have come to view strangers more as potential enemies than as potential friends. We keep our eyes on our luggage and pocketbooks as we travel. We may feel sympathy for the hitchhiker or the stranded motorist, but most of the time we keep driving. When we park in a shopping mall lot, we lock our valuables in the trunk, away from the eyes of strangers. We are often victimized by our fears, instinctively avoiding persons who look or speak differently than we do.

All our social institutions have been affected by the growth of fear in our society. Churches, once known as havens of refuge and houses of prayer, now lock the doors to the very persons to whom they claim to minister. Our schools now post guards to protect students from students and teachers from students. Drug-sniffing dogs and metal detectors have become standard operating procedure in many schools. Many office buildings and large companies have significantly increased security, some requiring registration of everyone who enters.

Certainly the statistics on violent crime over the past two decades justify a somewhat cautious approach to certain situations. Yet it is one thing to live with a reasonable sense of caution and another entirely to have most of one's existence determined by fear. Instead of risking new possibilities for ourselves and the stranger, too many of us continue hiding behind our walls, lamenting the world's condition. By failing to come to know the stranger, we too often make that person an enemy rather than a friend.

Visiting Churches

Most of us like to think of our congregations as warm and welcoming. Yet the reality is that our discomfort with strangers often carries over into the life of the church.

On three different occasions, Fred experienced significantly less than a warm welcome in visiting congregations on Sunday mornings. In one church, while seated in a pew with his wife, Fred heard someone whispering about them from four pews away: "Who's that? What are they doing here?" Fred, unintimidated, went back to the two people who had been whispering and introduced himself. As he walked back to his

13

own seat, he heard one of them say to the other: "And just who is Fred Bernhard?" In another congregation, he was actually asked to move out of a seat which a member felt was permanently reserved! In the third congregation, he had the experience of not being spoken to by anyone. Fred Bernhard does not, in Steve's opinion, appear threatening or intimidating – in fact, it would be very difficult not to like Fred.

During a tenure in church bureaucracy and years of consulting, Steve has visited a large number of congregations across North America. He has uniformly experienced enthusiastic welcomes from congregations when serving as a guest speaker or sharing a consultant's report. When his role and identity are not clearly known, however, the response has sometimes been very different. He has frequently stood drinking coffee by himself during the "fellowship time" between worship and Sunday school, while congregation members gathered in cliques. In one large congregation, he was even asked to mop a restroom floor by a pastor who did not know he was a visitor instead of a member.

Being asked to get out of "someone else's seat," being ignored by everyone else present, and being asked to mop a floor are not the kinds of welcomes which make people want to return to a congregation. To have such things happen is an abomination to the Christ we serve. We do not own the pews, and we do not own the church. Christ gave his life for us and also for the stranger we encounter in the church or in the community.

The drawing by Kimberly J. Haugh at the beginning of this book was inspired by Romans 15:7. People who journey to the cross welcome, accept, and affirm one another. The cross symbolizes both our ultimate acceptance through Jesus Christ's crucifixion and also our call to unconditionally accept one another.

In his letter to the Romans, Paul makes it clear that the Gospel is not just for the Jewish people, those who have been circumcised, the insiders. The Gospel is for everyone. In Romans 15:12, he quotes Isaiah: "'The root of Jesse shall come, the one who rises to rule the Gentiles; in him the Gentiles shall hope.'"

The Future of the Church

Many people are in the midst of a love-hate relationship with the Christian church. As Richard Kew and Roger J. White describe feelings toward their own Episcopal Church: "We see its warts and blemishes all too clearly, yet even while it infuriates us, we cherish it" [*New Millennium, New Church*, p. 89]. Some of us are bothered because the church is too slow to change; others are distressed because the church seems to embrace new trends and causes without regard for the role which tradition has played. Some are offended because of the church's involvement in what they consider political matters, but others are disappointed by the apparent irrelevancy of the church to the problems of society.

Ken Gibble writes in *The Messenger*: "It is no accident that we don't always agree on things – whether it be politics or theology or the church budget. For reasons God alone knows, God gives us people to live with who sometimes make us want to pull our hair out in frustration. . . .

"As someone has suggested, in the church we do not choose who our fellow members will be. And that's a good thing, because if we could choose, our choices would be limited by self-serving motives. Instead, in the church, in any true community, our companions are given to us by God's grace. Often they will be the very people who will upset our cherished view of ourselves and the world" [p. 21]. Loving the church means loving those who are part of it, and that is not always an easy task. Sometimes it isn't easy to love ourselves!

When our feelings about the church and brothers and sisters in the church are mixed, we can understandably feel overwhelmed about the possibility of welcoming the stranger. But difficulty in welcoming the stranger can also come from those of us who are pleased and excited by our involvement in the local church. Sometimes our needs are met at such a high level by the existing people and programs of a congregation that we have difficulty accepting change in what serves us so well. Having new members, however, means change for the church. Thus even those without mixed feelings toward the church may find themselves reluctant to embrace the stranger, without fully understanding why.

No matter how we feel toward the church, there is, we believe, no escaping the reality that we are called to welcome the stranger and to seek out those who are not part of the Christian community. If we wait to solve all of our internal ecclesiastical problems before we embrace the outsider, some of us will be waiting until the second coming. If we let ourselves remain so self-satisfied or focused on our own needs that we do not truly welcome new people, we will restrict the church's potential and shut ourselves off from the gifts God seeks to provide through new relationships. The persons who are at first strangers in the church may mean:

- more people for the bell choir.
- new teachers for Sunday school.
- less burnout for present members.
- friends to stand with us when life is hard.
- new perspective on our problems as individuals and the church.

The future of many congregations appears dim if persons cannot learn how to better appreciate one another and to celebrate rather than lament their differences. Growth for our churches is simply not viable unless we learn how to embrace those who are strangers. As long as we let our Christian walk be governed by the fears that grip the rest of society, we will find ourselves unsettled by strangers and unable to make friendship the normal expectation when we encounter new people.

Hospitality

The word hospitality is not new. We practice it in various ways as part of everyday life. At times, especially with those we already know and trust or know through others, we model it almost perfectly. We speak of southern hospitality and understand the meaning of a "Hospitality Inn" sign. We use the word to describe persons who exhibit extraordinary graciousness. Being hospitable is for some the opposite of being rude. The word also evokes images of tea parties, pleasant conversations, and an aura of coziness.

The meaning and explanation of hospitality, however, go deeper than those images. The experience and practice of hospitality lies at the very core of what it means to be a Christian. Its roots are woven into the foundation of Judaism and Christianity. An old Hebrew proverb notes that "hospitality to strangers is greater than reverence for the name of God" [Robert E. Meagher in "Stranger at the Gate" in *Parabola 2*].

In the New Testament, the Letter to the Hebrews makes clear the importance of hospitality: "Do not neglect to show hospitality to strangers, for by doing that some have entertained angels without knowing it" [13:2].

Hospitality is the **attitude** and **practice** of providing the **atmosphere** and **opportunities**, however risky, in which strangers are free to become friends, thereby feeling accepted, included, and loved. The relationship thus opens up the possibility for eventual communion among the host, the stranger, and God.

The **stranger** is any person or group not known to the host. The host perceives that this unknown person or group has the potential for relationship as an enemy or as a friend.

Hospitality is not something optional for the church. It is in fact the very essence of the church's life and witness. As you learn to improve your practice of hospitality, you will find relationships transformed not only with the stranger but also with those in the body of Christ you already know and with your friends and family. **Widening the Welcome of Your Church** means learning how to practice the biblical art of hospitality, to recognize the presence of Christ in the stranger, and to build transforming relationships.

Hospitality is not itself a strategy for church growth; but if you truly learn how to practice it, your church will grow. A congregation which practices biblical hospitality will be filled with passion and vitality and will develop a caring, inviting personality. Your own life will be enriched as well with new friendships, the joy of more energy in the congregation, and a closer relationship with Christ. People will be pulled toward you and toward your congregation. When members of a church start becoming excited about hospitality, others want to be part of it.

17

As you read and study the pages which follow, you'll gain an increasingly deep sense of what hospitality means and of its implications for your congregation. **Hospitality is not optional,** and the better you understand it, the more you will want to keep practicing it in the ways outlined in this book.

Remember, however, that hospitality is not always safe. There's a small chance that someone we choose to befriend will turn out to be manipulative or dishonest. We may occasionally extend hospitality toward those who will reject us. We may find that the practice of hospitality leads us into contact with persons we would otherwise have avoided.

And possibly the most distinct and frightening danger of all is that practicing hospitality may change our lives.

A Biblical Look at Hospitality

> **Concept:** The Old and New Testaments both regard hospitality as an obligation. The biblical texts do not question the worthiness of the needy stranger but instead examine the faithfulness of the one from whom hospitality is needed.

In contemporary North America, those of us with sufficient financial resources find travel an exciting and not overly difficult process. A person living in Indiana or Ohio, where the two authors of this book make their homes, can board an airplane in a snowstorm on a winter morning and be in the warmth of California or Florida before noon. Comfortable automobiles, buses, and trains provide other transportation options. Maps are readily available, and information centers can be found near many recreational areas.

Restaurants proliferate at an astounding rate, and so many of them are chains that one knows what to expect in a new city before walking through the door. Hotels and motels provide reasonably comfortable accommodations, and telephones and even fax machines in guest rooms make it easy to stay in touch with home. Those who want more variety and who treasure the unique can abandon the big chains and select bed-and-breakfasts and one-of-a-kind restaurants, but the searching process is still aided by the ready availability of directories.

The traveler in the Ancient Near East faced radically different circumstances. No one traveled unless absolutely necessary. There was no Bedouin Disneyland, and the concept of travel for pleasure or education would have seemed absurd. With the exception of a few cities, public places of accommodation were not available. In this environment, the practice of hospitality truly made the difference between life and death for the sojourner.

Hospitality in the Orient

People throughout the Mediterranean world regarded the provision of food, lodging, and protection as a virtue and sacred duty. The following were common components of the act of hospitality:

- **Bowing:** In receiving a desert guest, the host would often bend at the knees and gradually lower his or her body until touching the ground. This act revealed the host's desire to render the highest possible honor to the stranger-guest.

- **Feet-washing:** People wore sandals, and a day on the desert meant dirty, hot, and often sore feet. Washing the feet was an act of kindness which conveyed honor to the guest.

- **Preparing and serving food:** The host might devote considerable time and expense to preparing food for the guest. The generous Bedouins were known to deny themselves for the sake of the guest. The host's family ate later from what remained. The thoughtful guest always left a portion of food on the dish.

- **Needs of animals:** The host also provided the needed food and lodging for the camels of the guest.

- **All guests were seen as potential friends:** Obviously the stranger can represent a friend or an enemy, but the starting assumption in the Ancient Near East was that the stranger was a potential friend. Names were not exchanged until after the meal was eaten, if at all. An exchange of names and background information was not considered a requirement for hospitality.

The stranger could also expect protection from the host. If a stranger was being pursued by an enemy, the fleeing person only had to touch the peg of the host's tent to be safe. The pursuer would be forced to peer helplessly from outside the tent while the guest was entertained. That protection generally extended for thirty-six hours, the period thought to be sustained by a meal or the time needed for salt to leave the stomach. That length of time permitted a head-start for the fugitive. Psalm 23 takes on

20

new meaning when one thinks about the tradition of hospitality in relationship to these words:

> *You prepare a table before me*
> *in the presence of my enemies;*
> *you anoint my head with oil;*
> *my cup overflows.*

Abraham and Hospitality

Genesis 18:1-15 describes the hospitality of Abraham toward three men who appeared near the entrance to his tent. Biblical scholars (including Vawter, Von Rad, and Fretheim) agree that the three strangers are personages of Yahweh, though we are not clear in precisely what way. In *The New Interpreter's Bible*, Terence Fretheim offers this perspective: "From the narrator's point of view, Yahweh appears to Abraham at his home (v.1). From Abraham's point of view, however, three men stand near him (v.2). Yahweh has assumed human form appearing among the three men; the other two are angelic attendants" [Volume I, p. 462-463]. Consider the text:

> *The Lord appeared to Abraham by the oaks of Mamre,*
> *as he sat at the entrance of his tent in the heat of the*
> *day. He looked up and saw three men standing near*
> *him. When he saw them, he ran from the tent entrance*
> *to meet them, and bowed down to the ground. He said,*
> *"My lord, if I find favor with you, do not pass by your*
> *servant. Let a little water be brought, and wash your*
> *feet, and rest yourselves under the tree. Let me bring*
> *a little bread, that you may refresh yourselves, and*
> *after that you may pass on – since you have come to*
> *your servant."*

> *So they said, "Do as you have said." And Abraham*
> *hastened into the tent to Sarah, and said, "Make ready*
> *quickly three measures of choice flour, knead it, and*
> *make cakes." Abraham ran to the herd, and took a*
> *calf, tender and good, and gave it to the servant, who*
> *hastened to prepare it. Then he took curds and milk*
> *and the calf that he had prepared, and set it before them;*
> *and he stood by them under the tree while they ate.*
> **Genesis 18:1-8**

Abraham offers hospitality without being aware of the divine presence. That hospitality is consistent with the practice in the Ancient Near East and includes these elements:

- Abraham bows to them.

- Abraham offers them water, rest, and food.

- They accept.

- The meal is prepared and includes a calf, which would have been reserved for a special occasion, and butter, which was greatly prized by the nomad.

- Abraham waits on them while they eat.

- The strangers did not reveal their identity nor did they offer any gift or payment prior to the meal.

In sharing the calf and the butter, Abraham and Sarah gave far more than custom required. They chose to treat the three men as honored guests, and they did so without expecting anything in return. In verses 9-15, one of them tells Sarah that she will have a son. The fact that the gift of a child was promised can be seen as a response to their hospitality, but the promise of a son had already been made in the preceding chapter. The hospitality existed for its own sake, and Abraham has been lifted up as a model because of it. Had Abraham and Sarah refused hospitality to the strangers, they would have shut themselves off from the blessings God intended – not just the blessing of a son but also the blessing of God's presence.

Other Old Testament Examples

A full overview of all the biblical references to hospitality goes beyond the space or scope of this book. There are many other passages worthy of exploration. The following list is not an exhaustive one:

- Numbers 35:9-15 describes **cities of refuge**. These were refugee centers for Levites who needed protection from revenge until receiving a trial. They also offered safe

havens for strangers who needed protection from
enemies.

- In Job 31:32, as part of his **defense of his innocence**,
  Job speaks of his practice of providing food and lodging
  for the stranger.

- **Breaches of hospitality** are described in:
  - Deuteronomy 23:3-4
  - Judges 4:11-21; 5:24-27; 8:5-7; 19:15, 24
  - 1 Samuel 25:2-38
  - Isaiah 32:5-8

- The **provision of food** is described in:
  - 1 Samuel 9:22
  - 2 Samuel 9:7
  - 1 Kings 4:22; 10:5a
  - Nehemiah 5:17a

- **Requirements of the law** include:
  - Exodus 22:21; 23:9
  - Leviticus 19:10
  - Deuteronomy 10:19; 23:24-25

Jesus and Hospitality

In the New Testament, we find the practice of hospitality
directly linked to its practice in Judaism. As in the Old
Testament passages, the New Testament accounts do not focus
the issue on the worthiness of the stranger but rather on the
faithfulness of the one from whom hospitality is sought. Several
passages give helpful perspectives to us:

- **Matthew 26:6-13** gives an account of Jesus in the home
  of Simon the leper. Going to the home of a leper would
  have been unacceptable to the religious establishment,
  but Jesus does so without hesitation. While he is there,
  a woman pours a costly ointment on his head, showing
  a hospitality which foreshadows his burial.

- **Luke 14:12-24** includes the Parable of the Great
  Dinner, in which Jesus advocates that the one who
  extends hospitality invite "the poor, the crippled,

the lame, and the blind. And you will be blessed,
because they cannot repay you, for you will be
repaid at the resurrection of the righteous" [v.13-14].

- **Luke 19:1-10** shows Jesus again with one of the people
  the religious authorities would have avoided – this time
  with Zacchaeus the tax collector. A similar reference
  is found in **Luke 5:27-32** in which Jesus eats with
  "a large crowd of tax collectors" [v.29].

- **John 13:1-20** describes Jesus' washing the feet of
  the disciples at the time of the Last Supper. Jesus
  not only accepted the hospitality of others, but he
  also displayed hospitality through his entire ministry.
  The ritual or ordinance of washing the feet of another
  goes back to the custom in the Ancient Near East
  and is a clear affirmation of the value put on the
  one who is the guest.

The Least of These

Matthew 25:31-46 presents an account very similar in some
ways to that in Genesis 18, studied earlier. We are told to reach
out to those who are hungry, naked, homeless, or imprisoned.
When we show hospitality to such persons, it is as though the
kindness was actually being shown to Christ:

> *"Lord, when was it that we saw you hungry or thirsty
> or a stranger or naked or sick or in prison, and did not
> take care of you?"*

> *Then he will answer them, "Truly I tell you, just as you
> did not do it to one of the least of these, you did not do it
> to me"* [25:45-46].

Jesus in fact can be called the "Supreme Hospitalitor," for he
laid down his life for others. The writer's intention in Matthew
25 is to show the certainty of the end time and to answer the
question of who will be judged as righteous. Persons who are
hospitable to strangers are doing those deeds as if the other
person were Jesus Christ himself.

In this passage, Jesus makes it clear that we are not to reject the needy stranger like the son of man who was rejected and crucified. The stranger is to be welcomed, accepted, fed, and clothed. Welcoming the stranger opens the door to building relationships and developing deeper communion with one another and with God.

Our relationships with others are transformed when we seriously consider the reality that we are encountering Christ in the other person. That should affect all of our relationships, every day of our lives. The same principle of hospitality gets reinforced in these additional New Testament passages:

- **1 Peter 4:7-11** urges us to show love in all our relationships and to give evidence of hospitality. We are to "be hospitable to one another without complaining" [v.9].

- **Hebrews 13:1-2**, as pointed out in the preceding chapter, encourages us to show "hospitality to strangers, for by doing that some have entertained angels without knowing it."

Whether we think of encountering an angel in the stranger, as suggested in Hebrew 13, or the actual presence of Christ, as suggested in Matthew 25, there is no question about the importance placed on hospitality to the stranger.

Overview

Some common themes about biblical hospitality emerge from a review of the passages mentioned in this chapter and from other biblical texts.

1. Although "hospitality" is not always mentioned by name, it was part of the very fabric of the Hebrew and Christian people.

2. Abraham both depended on the hospitality of others when he was a sojourner and provided hospitality to other sojourners in his home.

3. Hospitality is often pictured as an expression of faith and of thankfulness to God who delivered his people when

25

they were strangers in Egypt and sojourners in Canaan.

4. The obligation to hospitality was in fact taken for granted in New Testament times. It was never seen as optional.

5. By entertaining the stranger or sojourner, we open ourselves to the blessings of God.

6. Hospitality is both a practiced act and an attitude toward others. We are to be open and accepting to all because God has been open and accepting to us.

7. The shared table brings together host, stranger, and God. The Lord's Supper (or communion or eucharist, depending on the terminology of your tradition) reminds us of our bonds with one another and also reminds us of the need to show hospitality to others.

The Oakland Experience

Concept: A rural congregation belonging to a denomination which is declining in membership experienced increased vitality and growth as a result of biblical hospitality. The same emphasis can work in any congregation.

If thinking about a congregation which has experienced rapid growth creates for you the mental image of a huge physical facility in the suburban part of a major metropolitan center, you are about to be disappointed. Those words do not describe the Oakland Church.

The Oakland congregation is located in an Ohio farming community. People there have access to urban centers, but you would not use the word urban or suburban to describe the church's location – you would use the word country or rural.

While most people would always have described the congregation as "friendly," there was nothing spectacular about the church's program of outreach. In fact evangelism had come to be a word with negative connotations for most in the church.

The congregation's denominational identity has likewise not been growth-oriented. The Oakland Church is part of the Church of the Brethren, a relatively small Anabaptist denomination, which experienced significant persecution in Europe. Evangelism and growth have never been central to the church's stated priorities or self-image. Like Mennonite churches and the Quakers, the denominational emphasis has generally been on peace-making, working for justice, and simple living. In recent decades in North America, the Church of the Brethren has been in a state of decline similar to what most mainline Protestant denominations have experienced.

Those in the Oakland congregation who would come for a meeting on evangelism would generally do so with their feet dragging and were more likely to come if a potluck supper was part of the evening. The reservations about evangelism which were held by the people at Oakland have much in common with the reservations experienced by many mainline Protestant and Anabaptist congregations including:

- Not feeling comfortable asking others if they are "saved." It feels awkward to make a transition from "Hi, how are you this evening?" to "Do you feel that you have the right kind of relationship with God? Do you feel assured of your salvation?"

- Anxiety over making "cold calls" on others. All people are busy, and many have difficulty getting the amount of time that they want to spend in their homes with other members of the household. Knocking at some-one's door without invitation and expecting that person to be responsive to talk about salvation and the church never seemed realistic.

- Inability to feel good about the oversimplification of the faith embodied in approaches like the four spiritual laws and other strategies based on the "right answers" to questions people themselves may not even be asking.

- The fear of rejection which accompanies asking someone in the family, in the neighborhood, or at the workplace to visit one's church.

From Negative Connotations to Positive Practices

Yet the Oakland congregation in recent years has enjoyed steady growth which has necessitated the expansion of the physical facilities. What happened?

- A crusade or revival? No.

- A new housing development at the back door of the church? No.

- A new minister? No.

- A new denominational identity? No.

What transformed the Oakland Church's life and, as a result, its ability to attract and hold new members, was an emphasis on biblical hospitality. The process began as the pastor (Fred) and the pastoral supervisory group began reflecting on Don Miller's article about "Brethren and Church Growth" in the journal *Brethren Life and Thought*. Miller's words about hospitality had great impact on that group.

We realized that we had in fact been practicing some aspects of hospitality but had not identified it as such. The actions were simply an outgrowth of childhood experiences and instruction for some in the church. As we began to look at ways in which we had already practiced hospitality, we suspected that those practices were largely responsible for the strength of the congregation. We wanted to better understand what had been happening in our congregation and what the potential might be.

The Oakland Church conducted its own survey of why people had joined the congregation over the past ten years. Responses indicated that the warmth and acceptance of hospitality were what had caused people to unite with us. When asked to share what impressed them most about the congregation, people made responses like these:

- Friendliness.

- A willingness to work together.

- A sense of closeness amid diversity.

- Everyone is important – each can be himself or herself.

- An alive, committed, faithful fellowship.

- A family atmosphere that shows concern and support for all its members.

What would happen, we wondered, if we practiced hospitality on a more intentional basis? We had no reservations at all about this approach. Hospitality not only felt comfortable and nonmanipulative to us; it also was fun!

Elements of Hospitality in the Church

As we began to become systematic and intentional about hospitality, we learned a great deal from one another and from the new people who became involved in our congregation. The following elements have all been part of our experience:

- We have emphasized that we are practicing biblical hospitality, and the Bible has been the starting place for our self-understanding and study.

- We've taken training seriously. While many of us have learned various aspects of hospitality during childhood and through adult experiences, the intentional practice of hospitality in the church requires understanding and practice. We offer classes or groups to train new people in the practice of hospitality, and we also have refresher opportunities.

- We give people assignments to practice different aspects of hospitality. Those assignments are an important part of learning the art of hospitality, and they are also important in being sure areas of hospitality are not neglected in the life of the church. The entire church needs to understand and practice hospitality toward one another, toward visitors, and toward persons in the community; but we also need to be sure people do not fall through the cracks. Specific assignments take care of that.

- We began at a relatively early stage in our emphasis on hospitality to see signs of the concept affecting congregational life. We began to see people lingering more after services. Congregation members were increasingly inviting friends and visitors to share meals. The volume of phone calls among members and visitors picked up dramatically. People began showing a special interest in the more fringe members of the congregation. Another important sign was a new attitude of acceptance toward those in the church who were not especially friendly!

- We had people prepared to invite visitors to their homes for lunch, an action which makes a lasting impression on those who come.

- We cultivated the art of listening as a part of the practice of hospitality. The deacons took several initiatives to encourage listening to visitors. We also learned to listen with more care to our inactive members, and we learned from them. The fact that we listened to the needs and concerns of visitors and inactives made them more open to hearing what we had to say.

- Classes and groups in the church began systematic strategies to reach out to those who had become inactive and to those who were potential members. What had been simply good intentions before began to become practiced outreach. While not every effort succeeded, the number which did was significant positive reinforcement for our efforts.

- In all areas of congregational life, we saw people interacting with one another in more accepting and caring ways. Evaluation and judgment began to be suspended. The starting assumption for people increasingly was that the stranger should be seen and accepted as potential friend rather than simply as an unknown.

- And yes, we certainly did experience numerical growth. During the initial three-month period of the hospitality emphasis for which we maintained records, we found Sunday school attendance went up by 36% in comparison to the same period the previous year and worship attendance went up 19%. We have seen increases continue in the years since then.

The practice of hospitality has strengthened our faith community at Oakland Church in our understanding of our calling. One person in lay leadership commented: "There is definitely an obvious challenge to our congregation: it is that we are all ministers, that we are all called." While that concept had been known to the membership in previous years, the emphasis on hospitality is what made it become real in the hearts and minds of many members.

If people are to be open to the offer of salvation, they must first feel accepted and affirmed by those who are part of the body of Christ. The church needs to be an open, receptive, affirming community where Christ's reconciling love can break down the walls of fear and hostility, competition and rivalry, and concerns about punishments and rewards. Hospitality creates that atmosphere, and our Lord can work through us in the process.

The Church Growth Movement and Hospitality

Most Protestant and Anabaptist congregations have learned much from the church growth movement. That movement has challenged us to examine the reasons for growth and decline in our congregations and denominations. Hospitality is not a church growth strategy as such. One does not practice hospitality in order to make the church grow. The emphasis with hospitality is on the stranger, not on the growth of the organization extending the hospitality and not even on the needs of the individual serving as host.

The church growth movement at its best has made us aware that outreach to others in the name of Christ is a central part of the work of the Christian community. Many of us had grown too complacent and had not thought about outreach unless our churches were beginning to hurt financially. Some of the styles of evangelism which have flowed from the church growth movement, however, have been aggressive, manipulative, and sometimes even degrading. The Scriptures give no support for approaches to outreach which manipulate others.

The church growth movement has often emphasized homogeneous groupings – helping the church grow by reaching out to people who are very much like ourselves. That is a strategy which has been especially effective in some situations, and a massive body of data supports the reality that most people who visit a church do so because a family member, friend, coworker, or neighbor invited them. Obviously we are most likely to interact with and to invite persons who are very much like ourselves.

The homogeneous orientation, however, has also been a limiting factor for many congregations. This is especially true in situations in which the typical member of the congregation is very different than in the neighborhood surrounding the church. Hospitality certainly doesn't reject those who are similar to us, but a person motivated by biblical hospitality intentionally reaches out to the stranger, to the one who is different.

In some of its forms, the church growth movement has sought to change people. Hospitality offers space for the stranger where change can take place. Hospitality does not require change before extending acceptance. Thus hospitality stretches us and pushes us to see others more as Christ would – to recognize the presence of Christ even in those who are very different from ourselves.

As warned in the first chapter, there are dangers in hospitality:

- It may in fact put us in contact with people who make us feel uncomfortable. Viewing all strangers as potential friends makes us vulnerable.

- Some people have a built-in resistance to any program, and those persons may not feel differently about one which makes hospitality intentional.

- We may fail to link the call to hospitality with the call to discipleship. Accepting the stranger or any other participant in the Christian community is not synonymous with condoning or accepting every aspect of his or her lifestyle or behavior. Ultimately, we welcome the outsider to become our friend and walk with us on the road of Christian obedience and maturity.

- Hospitality can certainly become ingrown, causing us to look inward to our own personal network of friends rather than outward to those Christ seeks to introduce into our lives. This has been a temptation in the Anabaptist tradition in which some have practiced exemplary hospitality but have restricted it to those already known or related to members of the congregation.

- Practicing hospitality can become artificial. If we let the emphasis shift to church growth as an end in itself, making hospitality just another program, the stranger will quickly perceive the self-serving nature of our embrace and withdraw from it.

Biblical hospitality, however, can push through those dangers and claim the rewards that come in truly embracing not only the friends we already have, but the strangers God sends into our lives as individuals and congregations.

What Motivates Us?

> **Concept:** The practice of hospitality won't transform your congregation if it is viewed as only one more in a series of programs to strengthen the church. The majority of the congregation must, at a fundamental level, come to feel that hospitality is a core part of our responsibility as Christians and come to share a vision of the congregation as a truly welcoming place.

- "But we've done everything we were asked to do. I don't see why the congregation isn't growing."

- "I went to our denomination's church growth workshop last week, but I don't expect it to make any difference. I've been to four of them in the last five years, and my church is still in decline."

- "I thought we did the right things. We started a new contemporary worship service, and we bought newspaper and radio advertisements. Everything has fallen flat. I feel like we wasted all our money and energy."

- "We got this terrific logo from our denomination and put it on all our bulletins, our church brochure, and our letterhead. I thought it would make a difference for us, but so far it hasn't."

The above speakers have all experienced the frustration of trying to achieve congregational growth without obtaining any clear results. Books have been written, workshops have been held, consultations have been available, and denominational programs have been attempted. Some of us have had at least brief periods of "church growth addiction," during which we've read, signed up for, or promoted every church growth strategy that came our way – or at least it's felt like that to us.

But in spite of all that energy, time, and money having been expended, many congregations are still not growing. Many which are growing are nevertheless failing to assimilate new persons as readily as they would like.

People can read the right books and attend the right events and still remain unmotivated to make the basic changes needed to become channels through which the lives of people and the life of the congregation can be transformed. Some people may say that they want new members; but when priorities must be set, they want their own needs put first. While we believe that hospitality is at the core of the change needed in a great many congregations, we also recognize that none of us can force people to do what they do not want to do. Shifts in attitude and vision are necessary to bring about increased church vitality and congregational growth.

The Necessity of Changing Attitudes

Creating a truly welcoming congregation is not just a matter of changing logos and developing new brochures for distribution. Logos and brochures can be a help in getting the attention of people and in interpreting what the church believes and does. They are rarely responsible for someone visiting a church and **never** responsible for someone continuing to attend and ultimately joining the congregation. Brochures are most useful when handed by one person to another along with an invitation to attend.

The pie chart on the next page shows the top reason given by people for their decision to visit a particular congregation for the first time. While factors such as the pastor's influence and the Sunday school account for some first-time visitors, the majority choose to come because a family member, a friend, a coworker, or a neighbor invited them to do so. No matter how many books a person reads on church growth or how many seminars are attended, the main way to impact the numbers of people visiting a particular local congregation is by asking people to attend! That's how it happens!

The influence of the pastor, of course, is of a personal nature. Those who cited a support group or another program did so in part because of the quality of interaction with other persons which took place through that program. Those who attended because of the music or the Sunday school have generally learned about the quality of those programs through other people. The quality of the interaction of church members and constituents with their family members, friends, coworkers, and neighbors and the willingness of church members to offer the hospitality of the congregation are by an overwhelming margin the major determining factors in people visiting a congregation.

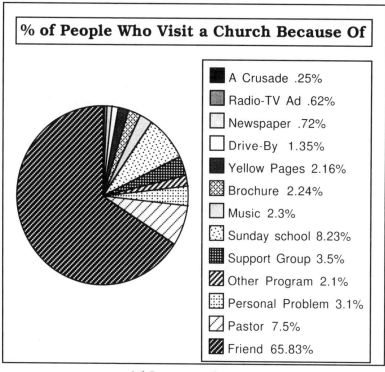

% of People Who Visit a Church Because Of

- A Crusade .25%
- Radio-TV Ad .62%
- Newspaper .72%
- Drive-By 1.35%
- Yellow Pages 2.16%
- Brochure 2.24%
- Music 2.3%
- Sunday school 8.23%
- Support Group 3.5%
- Other Program 2.1%
- Personal Problem 3.1%
- Pastor 7.5%
- Friend 65.83%

LifeQuest research project

Some persons maintain that the influence of television advertising for some large congregations is now passing that of one-to-one connection with people in bringing visitors to the church. While that may be true in some isolated instances, the message of national surveys through 1995 continues to be that person-to-person interaction is still the major factor for most congregations.

But what happens once a person visits the congregation? Even if the initial visit comes because of a television advertisement or for other reasons, people generally do not continue coming unless the quality of what they experience in the congregation is very high. That includes the quality of congregational warmth.

The chart below shares the results of a study in which persons who returned as visitors three or more times were asked to name the top three reasons for their continuing to return. The chart shows by bars the percentage of persons who named each factor as one of the three major influences on the decision to return.

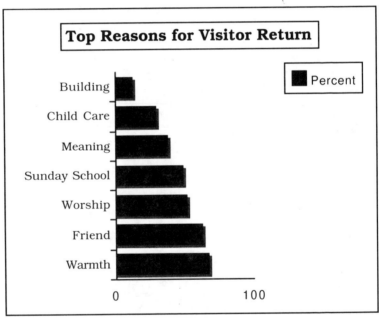

LifeQuest research project

Those asked to respond most commonly described their reasons for returning in words similar to these:

- "Because of the warmth of the welcome the congregation extended to me."

- "Because I have a friend in the congregation or made a friend during my visits."

- "Because the quality of the worship service helped me grow closer to God."

- "Because the quality of the Sunday school helped myself or my child grow closer to God."

- "Because my experiences there helped me in my search for meaning in life."

- "Because the child care offered was excellent, and I felt good about having my child in nursery and/or Sunday school."

- "Because the building is such a marvelous facility with many opportunities."

In addition to the top three reasons, people named a wide range of other factors including the variety of programs and the opportunities for service. The top two reasons, however, both relate to the quality of interaction with those persons already in the congregation.

Thus those participating in a study of hospitality, including those holding this book in their hands at this moment in time, need to remember that we are not simply talking about a change in program or strategy. We are talking about a fundamental change in attitude toward those outside the church and toward those who come to the church as visitors.

When faced with one who is not known or with one whose religious connections are not known, our immediate response needs to be one of acceptance and warmth rather than of evaluation. When others bring their friends to church with them, our response on meeting them needs to be one of acceptance and warmth. Like Abraham to the three unexpected visitors at the entrance to his tent, we need to (figuratively speaking in our culture) bow to show our honor at their presence and then offer to them the very best that we have (whether that is sharing a meal or sharing in a Sunday school class). We need a vision of the church as a truly welcoming setting and to see ourselves as extensions of the body of Christ.

The Place of Vision

In his insightful book *Sacred Cows Make Gourmet Burgers,* Bill Easum warns us that:

> *Failure to build a shared vision is the biggest mistake that gifted leaders can make* [p. 83].

The purpose of this book and the journey we are taking together isn't to travel back to the Ancient Near East so that we can literally duplicate what happened there. We don't normally bow to others as a sign of greeting. We don't slaughter calves for our dinner guests. Most of us don't see what happens to our food before it hits the shelf in the grocery store, and some of us are opposed to eating veal. Others of us are opposed to eating any meat at all.

We don't want to return to the Ancient Near East. We do want to bring the essence, the vision of gracious hospitality of the Ancient Near East and of our Lord and Savior, to our own time, our own lives, and our own congregations. We do not want any stranger to feel uncertainty in our presence. We also do not want a friend of ours to feel anxiety about acceptance from the rest of the church. We want:

- To show the honor and respect that was embodied in the bow of the Ancient Near East by our words and our warmth.

- To offer the fullest possible hospitality, including invitations to share in meals and to meet other persons in the household of faith.

- To reserve all judgment–and work on the assumption that the one who comes is a potential friend whose involvement will enrich our lives.

In the familiar Parable of the Good Samaritan, **Luke 10:25-37**, nothing is said about the worthiness of the person who was injured. No questions are raised about whether or not the injured party might have started the conflict or might have been drunk or on drugs. The starting point for the Samaritan is one of acceptance and compassion. The individual in need is not being evaluated in behavior. The priest, the Levite, and the Samaritan are the ones whose behavior is evaluated – and only one of the three has acted in an acceptable way as far as our Lord is concerned.

Think back to the other biblical passages shared in the second chapter. Again and again, we find that the behavior of the host is under evaluation, not the behavior of the guest. We are expected to provide warm, caring, welcoming environments to those who seek us out and to those we invite to share with us.

If this study is going to be fruitful for you and for any others who share with you, then it becomes of great importance to begin working on a vision of what it means for your church to become a place of great hospitality. What does that mean for your physical facilities? What does that mean for the initial greeting people receive? What would you want to experience if you came to your congregation as a visitor? You may want to visit some other congregations to experience what it is like to be a visitor.

Mystery and Curiosity

Are we frightened or intrigued by the world? Do the differences which exist between ourselves and others constitute a source of anxiety or of fascination? If we have been clinging to a world-view which is filled with foreboding, then embracing others within the church and within the broader society will be a threatening experience for us.

In *Further Along the Road Less Traveled*, popular author and psychiatrist Scott Peck shares this perspective on the place of curiosity in a mentally healthy life:

> *One of the things that characterize the most mentally healthy among us is their great taste for mystery and their profound curiosity. They are curious about everything: about quasars and lasers and schizophrenics*

41

and praying mantises and stars. Everything turns them on [p. 77].

Jesus spoke of becoming like a little child to enter the kingdom of heaven. As we all know and experience, one of the major characteristics of children is their profound curiosity about everything,

Why....? Why....? Why....?

We need to learn from children how to recapture a fascination with life and with the people whose paths cross ours. Our questions as adults should reflect genuine interest rather than a probing and evaluating attitude. We need to see fascinating, good possibilities in the stranger and also in the friend with whom we may begin interacting in a different way by extending an invitation to church.

The Place of Training

Unlike the case with some church growth strategies, most people feel good about the concept of hospitality and about learning to extend it to others. Most of us want to be welcoming. The majority of us, in fact, think we already are welcoming! But most of us, in truth, need to improve. **And we need to see that hospitality is not just another program – it is in fact the very essence of the life and witness of the Christian community.** When a church embodies that kind of hospitality, people want to be part of it.

If you are reading this book as part of a study in which you are sharing with other persons, then you are already well on your way to the creation of a more hospitable congregation. If you are reading this book independently and want to begin making a difference in your congregation, one of the most valuable steps you can take is to get others involved in a study with you, so that they are exposed to the same chapters you are experiencing and so that you can work together on the vision of a church which practices great hospitality.

Experiencing Hospitality
In the Church

Concept: The caring host provides the kind of acceptance and the opportunities which respond to the needs and comfort level of the guest.

Although she had spent all of her life in Charleston, South Carolina, Madeline moved to Phoenix, Arizona, following the death of her husband in a tragic automobile accident. She had seen an opening posted on her company's bulletin board for a position in the Phoenix office, and the idea of moving so far away from all the reminders of her husband felt like a good step to her. She was thirty-seven years old and had no children.

When she moved into an apartment complex in Phoenix on an unbearably hot June day, a woman in a neighboring apartment helped her unload boxes and in the process invited her to attend church on Sunday. That was quite a suggestion for Madeline, who had not darkened a church door since her wedding and had attended only a few times during her childhood and teenage years. Her life, however, felt out of balance; and she thought church might provide her what was needed. She had liked the neighbor who had pitched in so readily to help and wondered if there were more people like her in the congregation. She was also horribly afraid of saying something foolish or doing something wrong since she had so little church background. Her neighbor had told her that it was perfectly acceptable to wear shorts to that congregation in the summer. Shorts in church? That sure didn't sound like the churches back home. She wondered what else would be different.

Brad and Ann moved to Phoenix at almost exactly the same time as Madeline. They were both in their mid-forties and had a seventh–grade daughter, a high school sophomore son, and a daughter who had just finished her freshman year of college. Their dog, cat, and goldfish also made the trip, though there were a few goldfish casualties along the way. Brad and Ann had both taken new positions in Phoenix and were excited about the transition. They had lived in Portland, Oregon, for many years but had always appreciated everything in Phoenix on their vacations there – except the summer heat. Both of their new positions represented significant advancements, and they were thrilled with the 4,000 square foot home that they had been able to buy.

They had been very active in a congregation in Portland for the past ten years, and their pastor had already made contact with a church of the same denomination in Phoenix. They were hoping it would have as strong a youth program for their two younger children as they had enjoyed in Portland. Brad thought it would feel a little strange to be coming into a church as an outsider when he had just finished a three-year term as the chairperson of the church board in Portland.

Eddie arrived in Phoenix on the same day as Madeline; but instead of moving into an apartment by himself, he was sharing a somewhat run-down apartment with three other men. Eddie had just been released from a Federal Correctional Institution where he had served a five-year sentence on a drug charge. He was twenty-seven years old and had not finished high school. He had gotten a G.E.D. while in prison but felt that he had learned relatively little in the process. Eddie was determined to get his life in order, and the chaplain in prison had helped him reclaim his faith in Christ. He had a lot of bitterness over the length of his sentence, but he wanted very much to prove that the judge had been wrong about his potential for good.

Eddie had lived in Tucson before his arrest, but he had no desire to return to his old circle of friends in that city. He knew he would have to be careful not to resume his drug habit or to develop a problem with alcohol, which had really been his drug of choice until the time in prison. He had a job at a fast food restaurant and planned to enroll in a local community college. He had not belonged to a church before; but following his imprisonment, he wanted to become active in one. In fact he had promised the chaplain that he would be in church the first Sunday he was in Phoenix. He made arrangements to borrow a car for Sunday morning from one of the others in the apartment. Eddie decided to try a congregation that ran an advertisement in the newspaper which said:

> **All people are welcome here.**
> **Your past no longer matters.**
> **The present and future are**
> **what matter to us and to God.**
> **Come share with us.**

That sounded like the kind of place Eddie needed. It also happened to be the same church that Madeline and Brad, Ann, and their children visited that Sunday.

In the Shoes of Others

What a challenge and what an opportunity for a local congregation! Think about the needs the visitors just described have in common and also about the unique backgrounds which they bring to the congregation. They have in common:

- The fact that they've all just moved to Phoenix from other places and have never lived in that city before.

- The fact that they all want to feel accepted in the new congregation.

- The fact that this particular congregation may be considerably more casual than they've experienced in the past.

- The fact that they all will be interested in developing new friendships with people.

But they also bring unique needs and may well respond in different ways to what happens on Sunday morning. For example:

- Madeline has to decide how quickly she wants to let people she meets in the church know that her husband died recently. She wants to be open with people, but she also feels like his death is still far too painful a topic for conversation.

- Madeline has no interest in dating. She feels that she will need a lot of time before having

45

any interest in that kind of social life.

- Eddie doesn't want to date for a couple of months, but he is already looking forward to doing so.

- Madeline and Eddie both have had almost no past experience in congregational life. They feel uneasy about everything and are quite afraid of looking foolish to others. Neither of them feels at all sure about what happens in Sunday school. Madeline's neighbor has invited her to attend a class with her, but Madeline is a little uneasy about that. Eddie just plans to go to the worship service. His reading skills aren't good, and he fears that people may have to read aloud from the Bible in the Sunday school classes.

- Brad and Ann have had years of experience in the life of the church and are staying in the same denomination. While there will no doubt be some differences, they already have a good idea what to expect. They want to become involved as quickly as possible. Brad hopes it will be possible to arrange lunch with the pastor that week.

- Madeline no doubt still has a lot of grief work to do. A setting which will let her share when she feels ready to do so would be worth a great deal to her.

- Eddie feels lost about what to say to people about the years immediately preceding his move to Phoenix. How will people in the church respond to him if he shares that he's spent the last five years in prison? He wants to be honest with people, but he also wants to be accepted. He likes the saying of the church in the newspaper, but he also has to wonder if that's true or just advertising copy.

- Eddie has a very low income and is likely to continue having a low income for several years to come. Even a tithe of his income to the church won't be a lot, and he won't have much money to participate in church social activities.

46

- Brad and Ann are in a position to give substantial financial support to the congregation. Having served as board chairperson in Portland, Brad wonders things like what it costs to air condition the facility in Phoenix, what the pastor and other staff are paid in comparison to Portland, and how financially healthy the church is.

- Madeline is the only one of them who already knows someone in the congregation. She has the option of going to church with her neighbor if she wants to attend both Sunday school and worship, or she can simply meet her neighbor at one of the church entrances for worship.

When we think about hospitality, it's important for us to keep in mind just how different the needs of people can be and how different their levels of comfort in church can be. Church members are likely to differ in their own feelings about these visitors.

Any pastor and most church members rejoice to have people like Brad, Ann, and their children move into the community and immediately come to church. Most people will feel sorry for Madeline once they learn about her situation, and single males who meet her are likely to be frustrated that she has no interest in dating. Some persons will feel sorry for Eddie when they learn about his situation, but there will be others who are afraid of him and will wonder if he would ever bring a young person in the church into contact with drugs.

How would your congregation respond to the persons just described? These are all real people, and they all visited the same Phoenix congregation on the same day. We'll share more about the response to them later in the chapter.

From the standpoint of biblical hospitality, the church has the same obligation to be a gracious, affirming host to Eddie, to Madeline, and to Brad, Ann, and their children. There's a basic level of acceptance and affirmation which all these visitors should receive. As time passes, whether or not these persons continue to feel accepted will depend in part on the extent to which people in the church can respond to their various needs and levels of comfort with congregational life.

Think again about the definition of hospitality which was shared in the first chapter.

Hospitality is the **attitude** and **practice** of providing the **atmosphere** and **opportunities**, however risky, in which strangers are free to become friends, thereby feeling accepted, included, and loved. The relationship thus opens up the possibility for eventual communion among the host, the stranger, and God.

The **stranger** is any person or group not known to the host . The host perceives that this unknown person or group has the potential for relationship as an enemy or as a friend.

Some other words from the Ancient Near East and from Scripture may be helpful in thinking about the different situations represented within a congregation:

The **foreigner** referred most often to a person who made contact with Israel as a trader, traveler, or soldier. This individual would generally not cut ties with the original home.

An **alien** was differentiated from the foreigner and was a permanent resident of the community. Anyone not related by blood to a particular tribe or clan but permanently associated with it was considered an alien.

The **sojourner** lived in the community and had responsibilities, but the community was not fully his or her own. The sojourner's residence was temporary, and a return to the permanent home would eventually come.

Thinking about Eddie, Madeline, and Brad, Ann, and their children makes us aware of the differences in their comfort levels and their needs from the congregation. Now think about the needs, comfort levels, and expectations of persons in the following categories in terms of contact with your church. How do you and the church respond to:

- The person who is present every week and who has several close friends in the church? (This probably describes most people reading this book!)

- The person who is regular in attendance but whose closest friends are outside of the congregation?

- The person who attends only on an occasional basis and doesn't feel tightly bonded to the congregation?

- The person who has become chronically inactive and rarely attends?

- The visitor who already knows several members?

- The visitor who knows almost no one in the congregation except the person who extended the invitation to come?

- The visitor who has just moved to the area and truly knows no one in the congregation?

From the standpoint of biblical hospitality, we want as individuals and as congregations to make the warmest possible response to all those with whom we come in contact.

Appreciating Variation in Comfort Zones

A couple attended the Oakland congregation for many weeks without anyone in the church getting an opportunity to visit with them or even to learn their names. Their normal pattern was to arrive just as the service was beginning and to sit at the back of the sanctuary, as close to the door as possible. When the last hymn came, they were out of their seats and out of the door before there was any possibility of Fred or anyone else greeting them.

While respectful of people's differences in comfort zones, Fred likes greeting everyone; and his curiosity about the couple became overwhelming. He finally made arrangements to leave the chancel area early one Sunday and went out of the church through a side door. When he reached the door through which the couple always left, Fred found they were already out and running! He ran too and managed to extend a brief welcome (and good-bye!) to them. He was not, however, successful in getting their names before they left.

But they kept coming! They eventually stayed through the benediction and gave their name, but that was six months after they had started attending. Few people will wait that long to reveal their names, but some people are very slow to make commitments to Christ and the church.

In Phoenix, Madeline elected not to go to the Sunday school class with her neighbor, Sue, but she did go to church. Sue met her at a side door before the second worship service and sat with her in the sanctuary. Afterwards Sue introduced Madeline to four people (one married couple and two single people) who were members of the Sunday school class. Madeline was struck not only by how pleasant the people were but also by the fact that they did not pry. She volunteered that she had lived in Charleston for many years, and she found herself in an animated conversation with the couple who had both grown up in Atlanta and had visited Charleston on many occasions.

No one said anything to her that made her feel she needed to say something about her husband's death. Most of the conversation focused on life in Phoenix and the positive feelings the people had about the church staff and the rest of the congregation. Sue and the couple who had grown up in Atlanta talked about the possibility of having brunch together and invited Madeline to join them. Madeline felt comfortable accepting the invitation, and the four of them visited at the restaurant for such a long time that the manager finally asked if they could leave so the restaurant could be closed until the evening meal. During that lengthy conversation, Madeline did find herself telling them about her husband's death.

Madeline liked the fact that Sue introduced her to the married couple and to two other single people. Because of the circumstances which had made her single, she felt more comfortable in some ways with people who were married. She also appreciated the fact that Sue had not shared with the others the things that Madeline had confided in her during the unpacking process.

Brad, Ann, and their children also had a good first experience with the congregation. They arrived for Sunday school and
all went to their respective classes. A couple in the class Brad
and Ann attended introduced them to the senior pastor and the
associate pastor during the fellowship time between Sunday
school and the second worship service. Both the senior pastor
and the associate pastor had known that Brad and Ann would
be arriving soon because of the contact made with the church by
the Portland pastor, and they were delighted to meet them. The
senior pastor and Brad scheduled a lunch together. The
associate pastor introduced Ann to the education chairperson
who was immediately interested in all the years Ann had devoted
to teaching and to training teachers. The two of them made
plans for lunch during the week as well.

When they got into their car at the end of the morning, Brad
immediately grabbed his small notebook out of the glove
compartment and started making notes of all the people they
had met. He and Ann were already starting to feel like they
belonged. A couple in the Sunday school class with two high
school age children had invited them to go out for brunch
together after church, but Brad and Ann had decided to take a
raincheck because their high school son appeared a little
overwhelmed by the morning.

And he was in fact overwhelmed. He had met a lot of people
his age in the high school class, but he felt like it was going to be
hard to fit in with the others, who all seemed to be so close to
each other. The seventh grade daughter was enthusiastic about
the other young people in her Sunday school class and was
looking forward to the junior high youth group on Wednesday
evening. The college daughter had attended a young singles
class, which she had thoroughly enjoyed except for the fact that
it had twice as many females as males!

That afternoon, one of the senior high youth group advisors
telephoned their high school son to extend an invitation to the
Youth Supper and Forum that evening. The advisor offered to
have one of the senior highs come by to pick him up, but the son
decided to drive himself, so he would feel like he could slip away
early if he didn't enjoy the group. He in fact did enjoy the group.

Eddie was the one with the most misgivings about going to church, and he was the one who had the most mixed feelings at the end of the morning. Several people did greet him. He talked about being from Tucson, being new in town, and wanting to take some community college courses. One of those who greeted Eddie escorted him to a young man in his early twenties who was enrolled in a community college. They had a short visit, during which Eddie felt awkward. The visit was terminated by the young man's desire to say good-bye to the attractive visitor who had just moved from Portland with her parents!

While Eddie did not visit with anyone who shared a brunch invitation, he was surprised by two phone calls during the week. An elderly couple he had met phoned to say they had really enjoyed meeting him and wanted him to come to supper some night that week. Because he had to work every evening that week, Eddie had to decline; but he accepted their invitation to join them for brunch the following Sunday. Then he received a phone call from the senior pastor who asked if Eddie would be free to join him for breakfast or lunch sometime the following week. Eddie accepted the invitation and was more than a little surprised that the senior pastor of this rather large congregation would take the time to share a meal with someone so young whose clothes were out of style.

The couple, both in their seventies, who had brunch with him the next week made a real difference in his life. Eddie had been determined not to tell anyone about having been in prison. To his surprise, however, the couple shared as they were visiting that they had a grandson who was having so many problems with alcohol that they feared he would get into trouble with the law. It was clear that they still loved and respected the grandson, and Eddie found himself telling them about his own experiences with alcohol, drugs, and prison. At the end of the meal, they both hugged him and scheduled another time to eat together. Then he found himself sharing the story with the senior pastor, who shocked him by saying how much he respected him for what he was doing to turn his life around.

The congregation described did not handle everything perfectly. The college student to whom Eddie was introduced obviously abandoned that conversation too quickly. That was at least in part responsible for Eddie leaving the church with mixed feelings.

The class for Brad and Ann's high school son didn't succeed in making him feel completely comfortable the first time he attended. In fact, there may not have been anything the high school class could have done which would have made him feel completely at ease. The transition from one community to another and from one church to another is a major one and is especially difficult for someone who has already started high school.

The follow-up of the elderly couple and of the senior pastor to Eddie more than compensated for the hasty conversation with the other college student. Brad and Ann's son was mentioned to the youth group advisor who called him that same afternoon. All of these actions were respectful of the comfort zones which the visitors had.

Creating Places for People to Belong

But what happens after those new members have been coming for a few weeks? Their continued experience of welcome in the congregation depends in part of their becoming involved in small groups in the life of the church. A good beginning has already happened for the particular examples discussed:

- Brad and Ann and their children have all started attending Sunday school classes. Their junior high daughter and senior high son have both been invited to evening youth groups.

- Madeline didn't attend the Sunday school class, but now that she has met four people in it as well as Sue, she will probably start attending.

- Eddie is the one not yet pulled into a class or a small group. His initial bonds in the congregation are in fact to the elderly couple and to the senior pastor. These are solid bonds, but in time he also needs to be part of a group or class which has more persons in his own age bracket.

Some congregations are dependent on a multitude of different groups and classes for the integration of new people. Such churches often have men's groups, women's groups,

Sunday school classes, Bible study groups, prayer groups, task forces, short-term study groups, musical groups, and more.

A growing number of congregations are organizing the church around a total small group emphasis and involve every active person in a cell group. Cell groups then become a foundational unit of the congregation. When someone new visits the church, one of the first steps in assimilation is to start that person in a small group.

In the Oakland Church, every effort is made to get a visitor into a small group opportunity within three weeks of the first visit. This helps people begin to build solid relationships with others and can also be an aid to them in working through difficult faith issues.

Welcoming Strangers

Concept: While our culture teaches us to fear strangers, we also know that our best friends were once strangers to us. Life is transformed when we see the stranger as potential friend.

We've all received and extended advice about strangers. Most of that counsel consists of admonitions to protect ourselves and others from the harmful influence or actions of those who are unknown to us.

Statements and accounts like the following are commonplace:

- "Don't accept a ride from a stranger."

- "Don't go to the bathroom alone at the movies."

- "Don't accept gifts from strangers."

- "Don't take candy from someone you don't know."

- "Be careful of people who look like. . . . You can never be sure what someone like that will do."

- "Did you hear what happened to that man who stopped to help a person who had a flat tire?"

- "Did you hear what happened to that woman who let the stranger into her house?"

- "It probably doesn't mean anything, but I just had such an uneasy feeling when I met him."

As shared earlier in this book, we know that the world in which we live is not a safe one. Much of the advice contained in the preceding quotations is especially relevant for children. Yet we must be careful that we don't instill too deep a fear in our children and teenagers, and we need to avoid the trap of living in fear ourselves.

Our View of the Home

How we view our homes correlates to an extent with our attitudes toward strangers:

- Do you see your home as a castle with a moat around it and towers from which you can defend your property and those who live there?

- Do you see your home as a gathering place? Do you like to entertain?

- Do you see your home as a get-away or an escape from the pressures of life? Do you want to avoid bringing problems or controversy into the home?

- Do you see your home as a continuing work of art? Do you take great pride in the design, the furnishing, and the cleanliness of your home? Do you find yourself feeling resentful when other people are in your home, or do you covet opportunities to show people what you've accomplished?

- Do you see your home as Grand Central Station with lots of people passing through all the time – some of whom you know well and some not at all well?

An image of the home as Grand Central Station or as a gathering place tends to make us more receptive to strangers, whether we encounter those strangers in the workplace, the neighborhood, the grocery store, or the church. If your home seems like a castle or a get-away, you may be more cautious about encouraging people to call or visit you at home. Does that attitude extend to your relationships outside of the home?

There's nothing wrong with the attitudes toward the home just expressed. Most of us have feelings about the home which shift depending on what is happening in our lives. After an extended period of the home as Grand Central Station, we may start to develop great fondness for the home as get-away, though closing down Grand Central Station can be a tough job!

We need, however, to be sensitive to the reality that our attitudes toward strangers are formed by various influences:

- The things we've heard from other people.

- Accounts in the media.

- The way we feel about our homes and families.

- The experiences we've had.

Another influence can be how many good friends we already have. Someone who has just moved to a community finds everyone a stranger and is very conscious of the need to begin making new friends. Those of us who have lived in the same place for many years may already have so many friends that we don't feel a particular need for one more. We may wish we could figure out how to get more time with the friends we do have! Such an attitude, however, closes us to what we might gain from new friendships – and especially from friendships with persons who are different from us in significant ways. We may miss some of the blessings God seeks to share with us through new relationships.

The Essence of Hospitality

Our best friends were once strangers to us. There are valid reasons for wanting our homes to feel insular and safe, but those efforts do not always have the desired effect. By avoiding or locking out the stranger, we may in fact be locking out the blessings of God:

> *Do not neglect to show hospitality to strangers, for by doing that some have entertained angels without knowing it.*
> **Hebrews 13:2**

57

Hospitality to the stranger is assumed throughout the Old and New Testament Scriptures. Again and again, as in the Parable of the Good Samaritan, the questioning is not on the worthiness of the stranger but on the faithfulness of the one encountering the stranger. The Samaritan did not ask of the man who was injured: "Did you bring this on yourself? Were you trying to do a drug deal? Why weren't you traveling with someone else for safety?" The Samaritan simply responded to the human need which was encountered. The priest and the Levite who passed by are the ones whose behavior is called into question by our Lord's telling of the parable. Look once more at the core definitions of this book:

> **Hospitality** is the **attitude** and **practice** of providing the **atmosphere** and **opportunities**, however risky, in which strangers are free to become friends, thereby feeling accepted, included, and loved. The relationship thus opens up the possibility for eventual communion among the host, the stranger, and God.
>
> The **stranger** is any person or group not known to the host. The host perceives that this unknown person or group has the potential for relationship as an enemy or as a friend.

Whether we start with the assumption that the unknown person will be an enemy or a friend makes a difference! When anyone comes to our church or shows an interest in religious concerns, our starting assumption certainly should be that such a person shares with us a pull toward the heart of God. Such a person is a potential friend, perhaps sent to us by God for the enrichment of our lives.

Think how your view of the new person in your neighborhood, your office, or the church would be transformed if your starting assumption was:

> *This is a person sent by God who may be a great blessing to my life, or this is a person sent by God in order for me to be a blessing to his or her life.*

Obviously such blessings have a tendency to flow in both directions! How can we best show hospitality in the church?

What We Want When We Are Strangers

There are some important things which most of us want to experience when we are in the position of strangers, especially in terms of the church. Reflect on what it would be like to be a visitor to your congregation. Read this list carefully, and place a check beside those items which need more attention by yourself or by your church in order to provide a more welcoming setting:

_____ When visiting a church, most people don't want to be ignored. People expect those who are sitting near them to share brief introductions before or after the service or Sunday school class.

_____ When visiting a church, almost no one wants to be overwhelmed. Two-thirds of those who visit congregations for the first time do **not** want to be introduced in worship to the whole congregation. They prefer meeting people on a one-to-one basis. Introduce the new person to a few other people – not to every single person whose attention you can get.

_____ People especially do not want to feel ignored during a designated fellowship time. If they go to a gathering spot for coffee and donuts, they assume that some people will visit with them. They will feel rejected if church members are all in tight groups with people they already know. Be alert during such times for people who are standing alone.

_____ Visitors generally appreciate name tags for themselves and for the members of the church. That makes it easier to remember names and avoids awkwardness over names not being heard correctly the first time shared. Remember that you as a member only have the name of one new person to learn; the visitor has dozens or hundreds of names to eventually learn if he or she joins the church.

Name tags can also make it easier for you to introduce the new person to others in the church, whose names may not be as familiar as you would like!

_____ People don't want to feel as though they are being required to pass a litmus test. Most will feel resentful of conversations which make it appear that someone is attempting to do research on family background and church activity. Churches with a strong ethnic membership, such as those with many descendants from Sweden or Germany, for example, sometimes act as though those people who have last names that sound a certain way are more acceptable than others.

Remember that in the Ancient Near East, the name of the guest was not even asked until after a meal had been shared. While we exchange names at a much earlier time in our culture, we need to be careful that the process of doing so does not cause us to act as though the name makes more difference than it in fact does.

_____ Some people are anxious about how others will respond to certain aspects of their background. A person may be divorced, a single parent who has never married, unemployed, an alcoholic, or an ex-convict. These are not pieces of information they are eager to share.

We do not want in an initial conversation to push someone to fill in the gaps in his or her history. When we see an adult with a child, we should not immediately move to a question like: "Where is your husband?" or "Where is your wife?" It's better to let the other person share family information as he or she wishes to do so.

_____ People want to feel that others are interested in them and pleased to have them present. They respond very well to genuine expressions of delight at their presence.

There are many topics of conversation which are good ones with people you've just met in the church:

- *Ask how that person happened to choose your church to visit.*

- *Share how you became involved in the church.*

- *Ask that person how he or she feels about living in your community.*

- *Say something about the weather – it's trite, but it works.*

- *Ask that person where he or she is originally from (just don't stay focused on the question as though it's a litmus test or more important than it is!).*

- *Share something which you especially like about your church.*

- *Ask if the person has any questions about the church.*

____ Parents are always delighted when people show interest in their children. Direct part of your conversation to the child or teenager who is with the adult who is visiting. Compliment the child or teenager on his or her appearance.

____ If the person has an obvious physical disability, he or she will appreciate an offer of assistance if appropriate, such as information on elevator location for a person using a wheelchair or a walker. A person who is visually–impaired or blind may need assistance in moving from one place to another. Beyond such clearly needed assistance, people with disabilities would generally prefer that conversation not center on the disability (thus making it appear that the disability is more important than the person).

____ People appreciate directions to the sanctuary, an appropriate Sunday school class, or a gathering place for refreshments.

_____   ***People almost universally appreciate an invitation to share a meal either that day or at a mutually agreeable date later in the week. Few things show hospitality in a more meaningful way than having someone as your guest for a meal. Even if a person declines the initial invitation, the fact that it was given is still appreciated. Churches which focus on hospitality have a lot of people hosting others for meals.***

_____   People appreciate being remembered with a phone call the week following their visit. It feels good to know that someone remembered you and took the time to call and reinforce how good it was to have you present. That can be an opportunity to extend an invitation to a meal, a Sunday school class, or another opportunity.

_____   People appreciate returning the following week and finding that people to whom they were introduced remember them and are delighted to see them again.

_____   People who are insecure about church involvement or who feel uncomfortable in large crowds appreciate sensitivity to their desire to go slowly in getting acquainted with others.

Estimates are that between 3% and 9% of the North American population experience significant discomfort in large crowds. What appears to be aloofness may in fact simply be an unavoidable response to a large group of people. Such persons will often respond better to a phone call or a visit during the week than to a lengthy discussion in the middle of a crowd on Sunday morning. Very few people who experience such anxiety in crowds ever talk about it with other people. We simply need to be sensitive to the possibility that this could explain the behavior of another person.

_____   People appreciate literature about the church being shared with them. Brochures and newsletters can help answer questions at their leisure.

_____ Young adults and teenagers who come as visitors
are likely to dress somewhat more casually than
some congregational members. A compliment to
such a visitor about something he or she is wearing
(assuming the compliment is sincerely meant!) is
a good way to affirm that informal dress is fine in
your church.

*Of course it's possible that members of your church do not
feel that informal dress is satisfactory. That's a position
that many congregations, however, are rethinking. While
churches in most parts of the country have not gone quite
as casual as the Phoenix congregation mentioned in the
last chapter in which shorts are worn by many people,
a great many churches are moving toward more informal
attire. There are two factors behind this trend.*

*First, a large number of workplaces have moved to more
casual dress. That in turn has changed expectations
about the weekend; and people invest less money in
suits, ties, and dress shoes.*

*Second, many young adults are increasingly dressing
casually for all sorts of occasions. Surveys of young adult
males in 1994 and 1995 both reflected that 40% did not
own a suit or sport coat!*

_____ Strangers appreciate arrangements which make it
easy for them to know how to find the church,
where to park, where to enter the church, and
where to find things in the church. Clear signs
to the church, clearly–marked parking, clearly–
marked entrances, and clearly–posted signs and
directions inside the church help.

*That process can be made even warmer with a greeter in
the parking lot and a greeter at each entrance for the
Sunday school time as well as worship services.
Oakland Church has utilized parking lot greeters for
some time, and visitors have repeatedly expressed their
appreciation for that early welcome. Some churches have
parking places close to the main entrance reserved for
visitors as a way of showing that visitors are honored guests.*

_____ Visitors appreciate greeters and ushers who not only show warmth and genuine interest but who also have been trained to anticipate needs and to answer questions effectively. Ushers can often help by making an introduction to another person in the congregation.

Training for greeters and ushers is crucial. See the excellent packet "Worship Visitor Evangelism" from Net Results, listed in the Resources and References *chapter at the end of this book.*

_____ Visitors appreciate announcements and the sharing of joys and concerns being done in a way which does not cause them to be excluded. That means the speaker should always give his or her name, instead of assuming everyone already knows himself or herself. That also means giving sufficient context for announcements, joys, and concerns so that they will make sense to a visitor. If a meeting or activity only involves a small number of people, probably no announcement should be made in worship.

_____ People appreciate instructions for the service being clearly–stated by the worship leadership or in the bulletin. Is communion open or closed? Do people come to the front of the church for communion? Are persons in the church sinners, debtors, or trespassers as far as the Lord's Prayer is concerned? Are words for all responses and songs available in the bulletin or a hymnal?

The next time you go to your church, make observations from the perspective of a visitor to your congregation. You'll be surprised what a difference that makes in your view of the life of your church. You might also talk with some people who have recently visited your congregation and find out what they experienced.

Welcoming Children

> **Concept:** Children belong as fully to the Christian community as do their parents. Our Lord always showed special consideration to children; and we should do the same, which means looking at the life of the church from a child's perspective.

Jessica was seven years old and did not feel as enthusiastic about the move to Pennsylvania as the rest of her family. Her father was happy because the move from Michigan was the result of a significant promotion. Her mother was happy because the move put them only fifteen miles from her parents. Her younger sister was happy because Grandma and Grandpa would now be the ones providing child care; and her older brother was happy because his new school had intramural soccer, computers in every classroom, and other opportunities that hadn't been available in the small school district in Michigan.

Jessica had never made friends quickly and being made to leave the few close friends she had developed seemed horribly unfair. The family cocker spaniel, Betsy, had died just before the move. The whole family had loved Betsy; but Jessica had always lavished the most attention on the dog, who had slept at the foot of her bed each night. Now she didn't have Betsy to listen to her and nuzzle her and reassure her.

When they pulled into the church parking lot on Sunday morning, Jessica felt overwhelmed by the rows and rows of cars and the huge building. Their last church had been very small, and they could walk to it from their house. She normally resisted holding her mother or father's hand when walking, but she put a vice grip on her mother's hand as they went into the church.

The greeters talked to her parents for what seemed to Jessica like a very long time and then spent more time making comments about her sister: "What a cute, darling, darling little girl. We're so glad to have you here. You're just as beautiful as your mother."

Then, almost as an afterthought, the woman who was doing the greeting patted Jessica on top of the head and said, "And what is the name of this darling little girl? We're so glad to have you here this morning too. What grade are you in school? How do you like living in Pennsylvania? Did you get that cute little dress somewhere here in Pennsylvania?" Jessica would have answered the questions, but the woman just kept on asking them without giving opportunity for any response. Jessica decided not to bother, and then heard, "Well, isn't she the shy one? Not wanting to talk to anybody yet. Well, that's all right. You'll talk when you have something to say, I'm sure."

I'll talk when you shut up, Jessica thought to herself. She would never say such a thing aloud. She tuned out everything around her and hardly even noticed that her mother walked her on down the hallway and into a classroom for second graders. The next thing she knew her mother was prying her fingers loose and leaving her alone in the room. She turned and started to follow her mother out of the room, but the teacher put a gentle hand on her shoulder and said, "Now, Jessica, you need to stay here with us. We're going to have a really good time, and you have a lot of other people to meet. My name is Martha, and I'm one of the teachers."

The door closed, and Jessica's heart sank as she could no longer see her mother. She turned toward the class and saw twenty children staring at her, most of them smiling. She wanted to run but had no idea where to go. "Marian," she heard the teacher say, "come here and meet our new friend."

Marian walked up to Jessica, gave her a big smile, and stuck out her hand. "Hi! I'm Marian, and I'm glad you came today."

"Jessica," the teacher explained, "Marian just started coming to our church about a year ago, and she didn't know any of us when she started. I thought she could be your special friend for the next few weeks and help you get acquainted with the others in the class."

And Jessica began to feel better. She met more people than she could remember, but she got to visit especially with Marian and three others as they worked together on a play about the Good Samaritan. Four other small groups were also working on plays based on parables, and Jessica had a good time. There were actually three teachers in the room, and both of the other teachers introduced themselves to her during the session.

By the time her mother and father came to get her at the end of the Sunday school class, Jessica felt a lot better. It still wasn't as nice as being in her old church where she knew everyone, but she thought Marian might be a really good friend. Marian wanted Jessica to come to her house during the week.

Jessica was careful, however, not to appear too pleased to her parents. She still was unhappy about the move, and she certainly didn't want them to think that she'd had a good time.

And she certainly did not have a good time during the worship service. The beginning of the worship service was just as boring as in her old church, and she didn't recognize any of the songs. Then her father made her join the other children who went to the front for the children's sermon.

The pastor had a nice smile, but he used a lot of words that Jessica couldn't understand. "Be saved. . . reconciliation. . . redemption. . ." and something about "the blood of the lamb." Jessica had no idea what lamb he was talking about, and she sure didn't know why she should be thankful for its blood. She didn't want to see any blood – the sight of it always made her sick. In fact sitting there thinking about this poor bloody lamb made her start to feel nauseous.

Thankfully she didn't faint or throw up. That would have been embarrassing. What happened next was as bad though. She found herself being herded along with the other children out a side door of the sanctuary and into a room where they had to stay for something called "Children's Church" while the rest of the worship service proceeded for her parents. She kept wondering if her parents would be able to find her in this huge church building. Maybe they wouldn't. It would have been better if Marian had still been with her, but Marian hadn't stayed for church. Jessica was almost overwhelmed with relief when her mother, father, and brother finally arrived. They picked her up before getting her little sister from the nursery, so that was nice.

"Well, wasn't that just wonderful?" her mother asked Jessica. "You got to leave that boring service and have your own time with others who are in grade school. Wasn't that nicer than having to sit through the whole service like we did before? Just think how many new friends you're going to make."

Her mother didn't get it. Her mother wasn't going to get it. "It was okay," Jessica reluctantly acknowledged. "But I really didn't like the kids who stayed for church as much as the ones in the Sunday school class. I'd rather be in Michigan."

"Well, you're not in Michigan, Jessica," her father firmly said. "As a matter of fact, I've had about enough of your saying that you'd rather be in Michigan. We're in Pennsylvania, and it's time you got used to it. Grow up."

Coming as Children

Grow up. We all do grow up, at least physically, but that doesn't necessarily mean we grow closer to God. Jesus placed great importance on children and wanted to be accessible to them. Consider these words from Matthew:

> *Then little children were being brought to him in order that he might lay his hands on them and pray. The disciples spoke sternly to those who brought them; but Jesus said, "Let the little children come to me, and do not stop them; for it is to such as these that the kingdom of heaven belongs." And he laid his hands on them and went on his way.*
> ### *Matthew 19:13-15*

The Gospel of Mark has a similar account, in which Jesus shares this perspective:

> *Truly I tell you, whoever does not receive the kingdom of God as a little child will never enter it.*
> ### *Mark 10:15*

68

The Gospel of Luke shares admonitions about children and the kingdom of God which are almost identical [Luke 18:15-17]. Jesus does not mean that only those who received the Christian message while they were children will receive salvation, but he does mean that we must be child-like in our relationships with God if we are to receive what God wishes to give us.

As congregations, we need to welcome children in the same spirit which Jesus did. We need to welcome the children for their own sake, for the sake of their parents, and for the sake of what we learn from children.

Many congregations are not comfortable with the presence of children. Have you been in churches which:

- had several adults who complained if children made noise during the worship service?

- were reluctant to provide child care to make it easier for young parents to attend classes and other groups?

- gave relatively low priority to the recruitment of teachers and other children's leaders, conveying the view that those positions were not as important as property and finance positions in the church?

- had children's sermons in which the speaker really addressed the adults more than the children, sometimes in words the children could not understand?

- had difficulty recruiting people to work with children's classes, choirs, and small groups?

Some of those questions may be descriptive of what has happened in your congregation. If our enthusiasm for the presence of children isn't high and they aren't given a priority in our programming, we need to reevaluate what we consider to be important in the church.

What Do We Offer Children?

A recent study of "Children and the Church" shows that many congregations have work to do in being as supporting and

69

welcoming of children as they should be. Most of us need to spend more time looking at the church through the eyes of children like Jessica and also through the eyes of parents of young children. That study showed that far too many of our congregations have simply not evaluated their programs, practices, and attitudes regarding children.

The chart on the next page comes from the "Children and the Church" study and shows the attitudes toward children reflected in various program offerings and strategies in over three hundred Protestant and Anabaptist congregations.

Note that the vast majority of churches do provide child care on Sunday. Virtually all of the churches not doing so were very small congregations and generally had only one or two small children who were present. Only about one in five congregations, however, had child care available on a regular basis for persons attending midweek programs, classes, and meetings. Many said it was not provided because it was not needed. Unfortunately, it isn't easy to measure the accuracy of such statements. The failure to make child care available can be a self-fulfilling prophecy, with people simply not coming when it is not available. While many congregations do have a mature adult staffing the nursery or other child care, almost as many rely primarily on teenagers for that function. Repeated studies, however, show that parents who are visiting like the security of leaving infants and young children with mature adults.

Slightly more than two-thirds of those participating in the study had a children's sermon as a regular part of Sunday morning worship. Many of those, however, acknowledged that much of the content of the children's sermon was aimed at adults. Obviously adults can gain from what is said to children, but we don't want children to perceive that part of the worship service in the way Jessica did. The children's sermon, if a part of the service, should be directed at the children, keeping their needs and language abilities in mind. Adults will still gain from its presence!

About forty percent of the churches in the study offered junior church for at least part of the year. Junior church or children's church programs take children into a worship environment of their own for all of the worship service or for a part of the worship service. The most common arrangement was for children to stay in the sanctuary with their parents through the children's sermon and then to go to a separate area for the remainder of the service – thus sparing them the pastor's sermon and sparing their parents the challenge of keeping them occupied constructively in the pews.

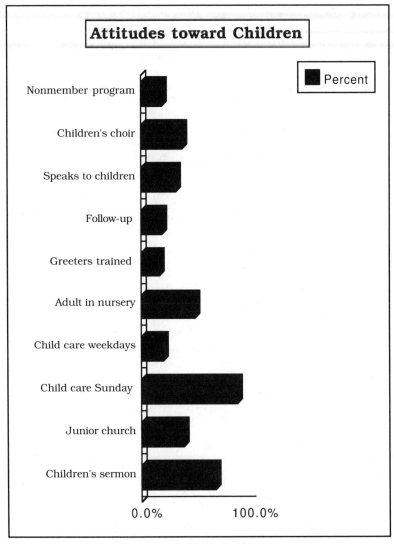

Data provided by Faith & Media

Some of those who participated in the study were philo-
sophically opposed to junior church, feeling that children gained
the most from remaining in the sanctuary through the whole
service.   Those churches often provided coloring books and
crayons or other activity materials for children. (Some churches
which had junior church also made activity materials available
for the portion of time children were in the sanctuary with their
parents.) Slightly more than one out of four churches which did
not offer junior church indicated that they wished to do so but
had difficulty finding adequate volunteers for that purpose.

Almost forty percent of the churches had a children's choir
of some kind.   Medium-sized and larger congregations often had
two or more children's choirs.   These choirs normally did not
perform on a weekly basis but were a part of worship once or
twice a month.   In interviews which were part of the research
project, those who had a children's choir indicated that attendance was generally higher on the Sundays the choir performed.

About one in five churches had some kind of program
through the week (other than day care or nursery school) which
could be used for outreach to children who were not already part
of the life of the church.   Some saw the children's choir
functioning in that kind of way because of the time rehearsals
were scheduled during the week, but several congregations
offered a midweek recreation program, tutoring program,
Christian education program, or other activity aimed at reaching
children both inside and outside of the church family.   These
churches were the ones most likely to report growing attendance
of children and parents on Sunday morning.

Fewer than one in five churches provided any training to
greeters or ushers in how to respond to children. Thus children
are often ignored or treated to the kind of head-patting which
Jessica resented.

Likewise, fewer than one in five churches had any
systematic plan for following up children who visited. There was
very often follow-up on the parents, but children were generally
assumed to be covered by that same process. A minority of the
churches participating in the study did have a teacher, another
children's worker, a child, or the parent of a child make a phone
call or another form of outreach to any child who visited worship
or Sunday school.   Those churches which did so were very

satisfied with the results and felt it had helped children who came as visitors feel more accepted and more interested in continuing to come.

Large numbers of congregations have some kind of day care or nursery school as part of the church's program or have a separately incorporated day care or nursery school which utilizes the congregation's facilities. Those which saw the day care or nursery school program as a part of the church's overall ministry were the ones most likely to report receiving new members through that entry point.

Strategies for Greater Hospitality to Children

Several clear strategies emerge as ways to increase the hospitality of the congregation both to the children who already are part of its life and to those who are visitors.

1. The church needs to evaluate the nursery and child care areas from the perspective of children and their parents:

- These areas should be spotlessly clean and attractive.

- The person in charge should be a mature adult with whom parents will feel comfortable leaving children. The need for this is in no way intended to be disrespectful of the excellent child care provided by many teenagers. Teenagers can certainly be part of the child care process, but parents who do not know the particular teenagers will feel better when a mature adult is present.

- Those who staff the nursery or child care should check with parents to know their names and to inquire about any other needed information relative to the care of their children. Ask what class the parents will be visiting during the Sunday school time so that it would be easy to find them in an emergency. Some churches even give parents beeping or vibrating pager units which can be carried and which give a clear beep or a soundless vibration if the parents are needed in the nursery. This can be particularly valuable in large congregations.

2. Sunday school classes (or other Christian education settings for children) should also be evaluated from the standpoint of children and parents. For example:

- Be sure there are adequate numbers of leaders for all children's classes. The younger the children, the greater the need for a small student–teacher ratio. This helps eliminate discipline problems, spreads the responsibility of following up on absent members and visitors, and makes possible greater personalization.

- Be sure the classrooms are clean and attractive – not only to adults but more importantly to children. Be sure that tables and chairs are an appropriate size for the age of the students.

- Have leaders teach the children how to respond to visitors. Jessica had a very good experience because of the way one class member in particular related to her. Introductions need to be made, and there should be efforts to help children learn the names of one another. Name tags can be a help if a class has the good fortune to enjoy frequent visitors.

> *Help the children in classes and groups learn how to extend hospitality to one another and to visitors!*

- Students should be encouraged to reach out to their own friends who don't have church homes and invite them to Sunday school and other children's activities.

- Respond to children who visit in a systematic way, either with a phone call or an offer to share in another activity during the week. Other children in the class can do this with middle and upper elementary. A teacher or the parent of a student needs to do it for younger classes.

- Some classes find it helpful to have fruit juice or

another light snack available.

- Leaders need to know how to respond to visiting parents – be sure they are clear on whether to pick up the children or if the children are to find them in fellowship area (if the children are old enough to do so).

- Leaders need to follow up on those who break a pattern of regular attendance. Though many cute cards are available for this purpose ("We've been missing you" accompanied by a photo of a dog or cat, for example), a phone call usually is a better follow-up procedure. A card or letter will occasionally be misinterpreted as being critical of the absence.

- Leaders need to get the name, address, and phone number of the visitors, so that follow-up is easy to do. This information may also be useful to others working at outreach if the visitors failed to sign a guest registration for the worship service (assuming that they attended the worship service).

- Leaders need to use a variety of teaching methods. Children need movement and change of pace if they are to remain interested in what they are studying. While it's certainly true that classes should be more than entertainment, there's no reason for them to be boring!

- Class parties are a great idea. Some classes also find it meaningful to celebrate the birthdays of students.

For more suggestions on creative teaching methods, the development of warmth in the classroom, and techniques for reaching out through Christian education, see **Reaching Out through Christian Education** by Steve Clapp and Jerry O. Cook (Andrew Center Resources, © 1994).

3. As already suggested, greeters and ushers need training in how to respond to children. Children appreciate being addressed directly in conversation rather than being talked about. Remember the feelings of Jessica! Adults who are especially tall sometimes bend or kneel to greet young children. Greeters should know where classrooms are for various age levels.

4. The worship service should also respond to the needs of children. Ways to accomplish that include:

- Having coloring books, crayons, or other activity materials available for children to use during the service.

- Having at least one part of the service which is especially focused on the needs and interests of children. This may be an anthem by the children's choir, a children's sermon, a puppet drama, or any other strategy which speaks especially to children.

- Those who do the part of the service especially directed at children should be taught to speak directly to the children, using appropriate words, but also cautioned not to "speak down" to the children or to use the children's time to deliver a message which is primarily for adults.

- The minister and other worship leaders should model acceptance and appreciation of children. When a baby cries, a worship leader might say: "The sound of children is the sound of a healthy church!" Those who serve as greeters and ushers should be prepared to give reassurance to parents who are obviously concerned about minor behavioral problems.

- In addition to modeling acceptance and appreciation of children, the pastor should also teach the congregation why children are important to the church and how they can be helped to feel at home. Adults should place just as much priority on learning the names of children as the names of parents.

5. The needs of children should be taken into consideration during any kind of fellowship time. In addition to coffee and tea for adults, be sure to have cocoa or fruit drink for children. Some adults will also prefer the cocoa or fruit drink. If your church uses "silent greeters" during the fellowship time to be sure that no one is ignored, instruct those persons to be alert for the needs of children as well.

Church leaders also need to model tolerance of the behavior of children during fellowship times. If children have been very quiet during worship services, they may have pent-up energy. If the fellowship area has adequate space, adults should not be upset because children choose to play games during the fellowship time.

6. Familiar faces are important to children! When class leadership is changed too quickly, new children may become disoriented and confused. Younger children especially need continuity. While many of us as adults like systems of rotating teachers and child care providers, those systems are not always the best for children who tend to like the familiarity of people they've seen before. It's also great to be present one week as a visitor and to be called by name when one returns the next week.

7. Being known by one's own name is important. No one likes to be known simply as "Fred's daughter" or "Mary's son" or "the youngest Stafford boy." Adults need to be encouraged to learn the names of children!

8. Discipline problems, when they arise, need to be handled with tact and consideration. How would you want to be treated if you were a child again? How would parents want their children treated? Obviously there are not always easy answers to discipline problems, but some strategies can help:

- Having a sufficient number of adult leaders often makes a great difference. A class of fifth graders that averaged twelve out-of-control children each week became a fun, reasonably-controlled fifteen when two adults leaders were added to the single teacher who had been working with the class before.

- Talking with children alone about discipline problems, if possible, is almost always preferable to doing so in front of the class.

- Appealing to children who are troublemakers
  to help create a better atmosphere in the class
  can be an effective strategy – that makes them
  part of the solution to the problem!

- Talking with the parents can sometimes help a
  class leader better understand the reasons for the
  behavior of children. Sometimes having the parent
  of a difficult child come share in class sessions
  for a couple of weeks can make a difference.

9. With children, as with adults, it's important for a quick response to be made when there is a break in what has been a pattern of regular attendance. That was mentioned in relationship to Sunday school classes but it's also important in terms of children's choirs, junior church, worship attendance, and any other children's activities.

10.   When a church has a day care or nursery school program through the week, opportunities should be sought for the church to show hospitality to those children and their parents. This can be an excellent port of entry to the church for those with no church home. Consider:

- Having the pastor share in greeting children and
  their parents on at least an occasional basis.

- Having a place for information on church membership as a part of the registration process so that
  you can be aware of persons who do not have a
  church home.

- Offering occasional parties or fellowship times with
  refreshments for children and parents. These can be
  an ideal opportunities for the pastor and other
  church leaders to visit with parents and children.

- Offering seminars on topics such as "Developing
  the Spiritual Life of Children" or "Creating a Secure
  Family Environment" to the parents of children.
  Have those taught by the pastor or by another
  church leader.

- Have low-key phone calls made, inviting parents to come with their children to worship services or to special events at the church.

- Consider having a different tuition or fee scale for persons who belong to the congregation! This rewards those who already do attend and can be a motivation for others to try out your church.

11. Be sensitive to children with special needs. Orientation for teachers should include alerting them to the fact that some children may have difficulty reading and should not be put on the spot in front of others. If students have physical, mental, or emotional limitations, some special arrangements may be appropriate. Special needs can sometimes be opportunities for innovative programs. Some congregations, for example, have begun midweek programs for children with Attention Deficit Disorders (called, for example, ADDventure).

12. Be alert for additional program opportunities which can help meet the needs of children. Is there a need for a midweek recreation program? A tutoring program? A Bible study group? A drama group for upper elementary children? Midweek groups can sometimes be an especially excellent opportunity for children to bring their friends who are not part of any local church.

13. Be sure that your promotional materials and strategies make it clear that children are valued in your congregation! That should be a part of a church brochure, of any newspaper advertisements, and of any special canvassing materials.

14. Involve children who are already in your church in helping you evaluate your programs. Get their input! What would make worship and classes better? What opportunities would they like? What help do they need in extending hospitality to others?

15. Provide opportunities for children to interact with older members of the congregation. Most older persons are in fact eager for positive contact with children. Those persons who seem to be crabby toward children are often that way because they have not had sufficient opportunity to interact with children in recent years. Do things like:

- Having children give flowers out to older members on a special occasion.

- Having a "secret friends" system between a children's class and an adult class.

- Having a children's class host an adult class at a dinner.

- Having a children's class survey an adult class on a particular issue.

- Having an adult class survey a children's class on a particular issue.

Welcoming Teenagers

> **Concept:** Teenagers are struggling for identity and coping with a multitude of pressures. The church's hospitality should offer them a safe place to be themselves and to grow in their relationships with Christ and other people.

Jennifer just celebrated her sixteenth birthday but looks and in many respects acts as though she's twenty. She enjoys the senior high youth group of a suburban Protestant church but considers herself considerably more mature than the other group members. Her relationship with Rick, who is a sophomore in college, and her part-time job as a clerk in a department store are both greater priorities to her than involvement with the church. She is concerned about her relationship with Christ but also feels that some of the church's teachings are too narrow for today. She has many homosexual friends, doesn't feel abortion is necessarily wrong, and has been having an active sexual relationship with Rick for more than a year. Jennifer's parents divorced when she was fourteen, and her mother has remarried. She spends most of her time at the home of her mother and stepfather but occasionally visits her father on weekends.

The same youth group has Diane, who is fifteen years old but, much to her regret, looks like eleven. She's very bright and also deeply committed to the church. Her views, unlike Jennifer's, are relatively conservative. She doesn't approve of homosexuality or abortion and says that people shouldn't make love unless they are married. The church holds top priority for her, and she's the kind of teenager most teachers and youth group leaders love to have – except for the occasions when her intensity and refusal to compromise make her a little hard to take!

Diane's mother and father divorced when she was nine, and her father has remarried. Her father and stepmother live in another state, and Diane and her younger sister live with their mother, who has chosen not to remarry.

Joel is seventeen, and his appearance drives adults crazy. He wears his hair long and likes t-shirts with outrageous sayings on them. His preferred music is heavy metal, and his preferred drink is Coors. He's fairly loyal to the youth group, but adult leaders can count on his taking the minority or unpopular position on any issue. Employment would probably keep him away from the youth group except that he seems unable to hold any job for more than a few days. At times it seems like he simply enjoys arguing; but he also displays considerable gentleness to people who are having problems. He really admires the pastor and will do almost anything the pastor requests. That same respect, however, doesn't extend to the youth group advisors. Most people do not know that Joel attempted suicide when he was fifteen.

Matt, who is fourteen, admires Joel and has an almost identical collection of CDs and tapes, purchased primarily on Joel's recommendations. Matt, however, is not comfortable with controversy and tries hard to get along with adults. Since he's more clean-cut in appearance, people in the church keep suggesting that he try to influence Joel's appearance. That, of course, isn't going to happen, since Matt would dress like Joel if he weren't so concerned about the approval of his parents and other adults. He seems to embrace the Christian faith and gladly helps with service projects, but his Sunday school teacher and his youth group advisor both wonder how deeply rooted his faith really is.

Angie, sixteen, has just moved to town and has started attending the youth group which includes Jennifer, Diane, Joel, Matt, and seven other teenagers. Angie lived in a rural community until this move and was very active in a small church which was surrounded by cornfields. She feels more than a little overwhelmed by her new environment but is trying to act as though she finds everything exciting rather than scary. She likes the kids in the suburban youth group but is still trying to figure out whether or not Joel means some of the far out things that he says. She especially likes Jennifer but feels as though Jennifer is already too involved with other people to make much time for a new friendship. The church has always been very important to Angie, and she's looking forward to the summer work trip that's being planned.

Understanding Teenagers Today

Although the names have been changed, all five of the young people just described are members of the same youth group. They reflect the kind of diversity which adult leaders are finding in youth groups around North America. These are teens who aren't going to agree on everything, but they are also capable of extending significant support to each other.

There has probably never been an easy day to be a teenager, and our present day is no exception. Consider these aspects of life for today's young people:

1. More young people than ever spend at least part of their childhood in a single parent home, and many others divide their time between two households: one with a mother and stepfather and one with a father and stepmother. Children of different marriages also get mixed in the households.

2. Teenagers continue to be heavily influenced by the media, with many spending around twenty-five hours a week watching television. Computers and the Internet have also had powerful influence on today's teens. The Internet brings access to all sorts of information and also makes possible the development of relationships with persons in other parts of the country or the world. Teens are also comfortable with computers and the Internet in a way that many adults are not.

3. Music pervades the culture of teenagers with heavy metal, rock, country-western, and alternative all having considerable influence. While the music of one generation has not always sat well with other generations, parents today do seem to have more openness to and appreciation of the music of their teenage children than some past generations have had. It continues to be difficult to truly understand teens without understanding at least some of their music.

4. Teens are being raised in an extremely materialistic, money-conscious culture. Adult society has done an excellent job teaching youth some very questionable values: that people who earn more money are better people than those who are poor; that the primary standard for evaluating success is financial; that the purpose of getting an education is to get a job to earn more money; and that one's own financial needs come before the needs of others.

Many young people are hearing all those messages about affluence but are themselves growing up in poverty. Black youth are at least four times more likely than white youth to be in families with incomes below the poverty level, and Native American youth are twice again as likely to be in poverty situations. Poor youth, however, are very often not involved in churches.

Youth of all economic backgrounds are more likely than ever to have part-time employment during the school year and full-time employment during the summer months. Many fast-food restaurants are heavily dependent on the teenage employees whom they pay minimum wage or only a little more. The major use of money from part-time and summer employment is in the provision of an automobile.

5. Birth control and abortion are both more readily available to teens than in some past generations. Among sixth graders, the percentage who are sexually active is about 7%; and that percentage keeps rising through the twelfth grade, when around 60% of teens are involved in sexually–active relationships. While a few churches teach more about sexual values, beliefs, practices, and decision-making than in some past generations, most deal very little with the topic except to encourage abstinence. Abstinence is certainly desirable, but most teens need for such teaching to be rooted in a fuller discussion of human sexuality from a biblical perspective.

6. Teenagers today, as in every generation, are heavily influenced by their peers. In many respects they care more about the approval of people their own age than of their parents and other adults. Many teens demonstrate significant caring for one another, but many others feel isolated.

7. Teens today are more likely to be the victims of crime and the agents of crime alike. Some estimates place the percentage of teens who have committed theft at 10% and the percentage who have been involved in significant fighting at 28%. Most communities are locking up larger and larger numbers of teenagers, often without doing anything to lower the crime rate. Incarceration generally hardens teens and puts them under the influence of more experienced criminals.

8. Teens are often the victims of physical or sexual abuse. The percentage who are abused increases steadily with age. Among sixth grade males, around 14% have been physically or sexually abused; the percentage for sixth grade females is 18%. By the eleventh grade, the percentage for males has gone up to 17% and for girls all the way to 35%. Abuse also makes it about twice as likely that teens will suffer depression, lose self-esteem, and feel that they are under continuous stress.

9. Widespread availability of alcohol and other drugs continues to be the case across North America. Percentages reported differ from study to study, but all show that abuse of alcohol stands as a far greater problem than the abuse of any illegal drugs. As many as 31% of teenagers may drink to excess, and around 11% experiment with drugs. In certain communities, those percentages may run much higher. [See, in particular, Peter Benson's *The Troubled Journey*, listed in the *Resources and References* chapter.]

10. Teens today are also more likely than ever to have problems with depression and, like Joel, to have attempted suicide. At least 15% have experienced serious depression, and estimates of those attempting suicide range from 5% to 13%.

11. But there's another side to teenagers today which is too often overlooked and under-publicized! For example:

- Teens are interested in spiritual matters. Gallup polls and other studies show that teens continue to be interested in spiritual life retreats.

- Teens like to do things for others. Service projects are very attractive to teens, and participation in them correlates strongly with lower levels of early sexual activity and lower levels of criminal activity.

- Teens care about their parents and continue to do so following divorces. While teens are almost unanimous in not liking divorce, they don't stop loving their parents because of it.

- While all teens seek improvement, most are relatively happy with their lives.

- The kind of youth who tend to be active in our congregations are not as frequently in "at risk" categories as other teens.

What It Means To Welcome Youth

What does it mean for the church to provide a welcoming place for young people like Jennifer, Diane, Joel, Matt, and Angie? Churches which help young people feel at home tend to be characterized by several things:

- **Welcoming congregations appreciate the fact that youth are not just the "church of tomorrow" but are in fact part of the church today.** They recognize the desire of young people to make a difference in the lives of others and provide them with opportunities to do so, not only with summer mission trips but also with late afternoon, evening, or weekend service projects. They also encourage young people to be active on boards and committees of the church, often inviting them to serve in pairs for mutual support.

- **Welcoming congregations recognize that it is crucial to provide an accepting atmosphere for teens**, regardless of superficial matters such as hair-style and clothing. Adults who work with teens need to be helped to recognize that clothes and hair are not appropriate issues for argument in the Christian community.

- **Welcoming congregations take very seriously the need to provide a "safe place" for youth.** They insist that adults who work with teens and the teens themselves honor confidentiality and respect differences. Although some good-natured kidding may take place, it's important that neither Diane nor Joel, for example, be criticized or made the

victim of brutal jokes because of their differences
from others in the group. Both Diane's quick
agreement with adult opinions and readiness to help
and Joel's reluctance to share agreement or help can
subject them to criticism.

The need for confidentiality can run deeper. What
Jennifer says about sexual activity or what Joel
confesses about drinking should not be spread
outside the group. There may be instances when a
youth leader is sufficiently concerned about the
danger of suicide to feel that something must be
shared with a parent, but such instances should
and must be very rare – or people will not share
what they really think and feel with the group.

- **Welcoming congregations offer a balance of
  opportunities for youth** but also recognize that some
  teens will be more comfortable with one or two kinds
  of activities than with others. Give youth permission
  to "pick and choose."

  - Youth should have the opportunity to share
    in **worship** and to give leadership to congregational
    services. Youth choirs and other music groups
    can also be valuable opportunities.

  - Youth also need **learning** opportunities. They
    need to learn about the Bible and about how
    to apply those ancient teachings to contemporary
    life.

  - **Recreation and social** opportunities are also
    quite important. Some church youth programs
    are criticized for being "nothing but fun," but
    such activities are a major part of building group
    identity and also provide valuable ports of entry
    for new young people. Encourage group members
    to bring guests on movie nights, on weekend
    retreats, to ski trips, and on summer trips.

  - **Service** opportunities are also important. Those
    can take many forms including improvements to
    the church, help to senior citizens with home and

87

yard work, the rehabilitation of neglected properties, working with a food pantry, and summer work trips to mission sites.

- **Welcoming congregations teach youth about hospitality** – how to show it to one another, to new youth like Angie, and to adults.

- **Welcoming congregations appreciate the role food can play for youth** just as it does for adults. Refreshments at youth group meetings, good food for overnight lock-ins and retreats, pizza parties to welcome new members, and meals shared between adult leaders and youth can all be part of a welcoming group atmosphere.

- **Welcoming congregations have had considerable success with mentoring programs** in which adults are paired with youth. The adult and the teenager meet together at least once a month to talk about things of concern to both of them and particularly to work on questions of values and beliefs.

- **Welcoming congregations have learned the crucial role which small group sharing should play in youth work.** Larger youth groups need to have enough adult leaders to make it possible for some discussions to happen in small groups. Youth groups tend to level off at an average attendance of 25 no matter how great the potential number may be.

Welcoming Young Adults

> **Concept:** Almost all churches want to reach more young adults, especially young adult families. Making young adults part of the church, however, either requires change or causes change.

"That drama that was done at worship last week would have been just fine for some kind of evening program," said Helen Adams, who was fifty-three years old and president of the Kum Dubble class at Cedar Creek Community Church. Although not herself a member of the church board, she was speaking at their meeting by request of the class. "What we don't understand is why it was part of the worship service and replaced the sermon. Along with that, we're very concerned about the songs that we've been singing from that new loose-leaf hymnal. They simply do not sound worshipful."

"Helen, those are part of the changes that the worship committee talked to the congregation about at the annual meeting," responded Bill Avery, who was chairperson of that committee. "We've been careful to just do one song a week from the loose-leaf hymnal, and we've intentionally only done the drama once a month. Everyone seemed to like the drama last month, and no one complained about it replacing the sermon. Was there something different about this one?"

"Speaking only for myself and not for the class, this one was not as uplifting. The first drama that was done emphasized the place of forgiveness in our lives, and there was something to get out of that even without a sermon. This one seemed almost entirely about AIDS; and to tell you the truth, all it did was make us feel bad. At least that's all it did for me. There are people who come to worship who are going through very difficult times in their own lives. Mrs. Bartholomew lost her husband just two weeks ago, and Walt Adams was just released from the hospital. What was there in the drama for them? A sermon, on the other hand, usually has at least something which you can grab hold of to get you through the week, to recharge you in a sense. This one didn't do that."

"I agree that this drama was a little heavier than the first one," said Sam Walters, the pastor. "What the drama was trying to show, however, is the way that God's strength and help come to people in the midst of difficult times. The central figure in the drama did have AIDS, but I didn't see the drama being primarily about AIDS. I don't apologize for the fact that AIDS was part of it, because that's a part of contemporary life which we need to face. I saw the emphasis of the drama, however, being on the courage of the man who had the terminal illness and on the support he received from his faith and from the friendship of others. I would think that might have been helpful to Mrs. Bartholomew and to Walt Adams."

"As a matter of fact," Bill Avery offered, "I heard Walt Adams say that he appreciated the drama."

"Well, I certainly didn't mean to be speaking for him," Helen responded, "but I know that Mrs. Bartholomew was quite upset. She told me that she was."

"Then I'll certainly make a point to call on her this week," said Sam, "and I do appreciate your calling that to my attention."

"Pastor Sam," Helen continued, "I am truly grateful for all the hard work you've done for our congregation, and I think the others in the Kum Dubble class agree with me. But when we were talking about some changes coming to worship, you said that one of the major reasons was to try and reach young adults. We've been using the new hymnal for two months now, and we've had two dramas instead of sermons. Where are the new young adults? I don't see them coming!"

"Have you invited any to come yourself?" asked Barb Wolinski, who chaired the membership commission. "Remember, that was part of the plan. All of us have been encouraged to invite the people we know, especially young adults."

"No, I haven't," answered Helen. "I don't know that many

young adults; and quite frankly, I don't feel good enough about what is happening in our services to invite anyone I do know. Barb, you're one of the few young adults active in our congregation. We're dependent on people like you to invite others your age."

"My husband and I have invited another couple, as a matter of fact," said Barb. "They came to the first service that had a drama in it, and they returned two more times. They've been gone or had company the last couple of weekends so they weren't here for this drama."

"You mean the nice young couple who had a little girl with them and sat right between you and your husband?" Helen asked.

"Yes," answered Barb.

"Well, I hadn't realized those were prospective members. The way you and your husband with interacting with them and the way your husband kept their daughter on his lap through the service, I just assumed that they were relatives of yours. But those must have been the only ones so far."

"Yes," agreed Sam. "Those probably are the only ones so far. We all need to be inviting more people. I think it is true that some of us don't know a lot of young adults who aren't already involved in a church somewhere else in town. But I think a greater problem is that we often don't feel comfortable talking about our faith and the church. We're planning to have some small groups during Lent to help us all become more comfortable reaching out to others."

"Then there doesn't seem to be a lot of point in continuing to do different things in worship if it will be Lent before we have the training for the next step in outreach," argued Helen.

"Some of us," Barb said, striving hard to keep the irritation out of her voice, "are going to be inviting more people. What we are doing is creating a more contemporary environment for the people we do get to visit. Drama speaks much more effectively to some people my age than a sermon. No offense to you, Sam, but that just isn't my favorite medium. I'm glad the sermon does help others, and I wouldn't want drama every week if that was going to be hard on Mrs. Bartholomew or Helen or anyone else. We need some drama, though, to help younger people feel it's worthwhile to connect with us here. And then the songs, Helen. I don't want to be offensive, but some of the hymns that mean a lot to you don't speak to me at all. What about 'Are Ye Able?' That one gets me every time. We sing back 'Yes, we are able,' when we know that we're not. The traditional hymns that we sing and the music that the organist plays are actually not the favorite kind of music for most of the population. Only about 4% of the public prefer classical and organ music."

Helen sighed. "This is more complicated than I'd thought. Now I see why Sam tried to get us to consider starting a second service so that one could be traditional and the other contemporary. It's hard to mix the two. I know that we need new members; I just wish there was another way to do it."

Young Adult Perspectives

Virtually all congregations want more members, and most have a special desire to reach those in the young adult years (18-35). Many older members, however, end up feeling like Helen: they want to reach new members but aren't especially enthused about the changes which are part of that process.

And change is part of the process of growth, especially when the church seeks young adults. Most churches have to go through change in order to attract and involve young adults; but even if more young adults are reached without significant change, their presence in the life of the church will itself cause change!

The meeting described at the beginning of this chapter took place in a congregation in the southeastern part of the United States, but similar conversations have occurred many other places. Sharing that example is not meant to convey that more contemporary worship services are always necessary to reach young adults, but changes in worship are certainly a significant part of what is happening in many congregations around North America. It's also important to note that there are some twenty-two-year-olds who prefer traditional music and some fifty-three-year-olds who prefer contemporary sounds. The generalizations, however, do tend to hold in most congregations.

Consider some of the ways in which the perspective of young adults may differ from that of older adults in the church:

1. Young adults are more likely to appreciate more con-temporary worship services. Young adults are not as likely as older adults to appreciate the traditional hymns, classical anthems, and organ music of most local churches. This is especially true for those young adults who did not grow up involved in a local congregation.

Although truly great preaching tends to influence most people, ministers can have an especially difficult time making the connection with young adults. (There's also a shortage of truly great preaching, but that's a topic for another book!) Young adults have, for the most part, been raised in a television and computer-oriented society in which the attention spans required on any given topic are relatively short. A sermon can require as much as thirty or forty minutes of undivided attention. The sermon as a medium simply does not hold attention as well as a medium like drama or video. Increasing numbers of churches are using drama or video instead of the sermon or are using drama or video to enhance the message of the sermon.

2. Young adults tend to be more informal about church. As discussed in the chapter *Welcoming Strangers*, casual clothing has become more common at work and in the church, especially among young adults. Some congregations intention-ally ask ushers to dress in a variety of ways as a visual message to visitors that they should feel free to dress however they wish.

3. Troubles with the justice system are part of life for some young adults. The problem, in fact, is perhaps not as much that young adults today are committing more criminal acts than in the past, but rather than law enforcement authorities are so much more vigorous in their prosecution of offenders. A young adult today arrested for a crime is **three or four times** more likely to be incarcerated for it than his or her boomer counterpart ten years ago. That person is also more likely to be locked up for a nonviolent crime. Currently more than one out of four young adult black men is in prison, on probation, or on parole. That's more than are enrolled in college.

The United States locks up more people per hundred thousand population than any other country in the world, including South Africa. [Information shared here comes from the U.S. Department of Justice.]

When we talk with young adults about church membership, we are more likely than in the past to encounter some who have had very unpleasant experiences with law enforcement. That doesn't mean they won't respond positively to the church – the question is how the church will respond to them. Remember that in the hospitality practiced in the Ancient Near East, the burden was always on the host rather than on the guest.

4. Financial prospects for young adults today may not be as positive as in some past generations. While many new jobs have been created in recent years, a depressing number of them are in minimum wage and part-time positions. College graduates still do much better than others, but the opportunities are not as good in many fields. The cost of a college education has also skyrocketed at the same time that grants and scholarships have become harder to obtain. Increasing numbers of college and trade school students must rely on borrowing money to complete college, and that debt hangs over them for years.

The percentage of young adults owning homes has decreased since the early seventies, as shown in the first chart on the next page. For a variety of economic reasons, rental housing has also become more expensive in some parts of the country. [In part, tax laws in the early eighties lowered some of the incentives for investing in rental housing by making rental unit owners depreciate their properties in different ways. This has caused them to make fewer investments in rental housing and to want to recover more money as they rent the housing which they already own.] One of the results of this situation is that a larger percentage of young adults in the 18-24 year-old range are living with their parents or other relatives than in the past. Finances have understandably become a greater priority for young adults. The second chart shows how goals of college freshmen have changed.

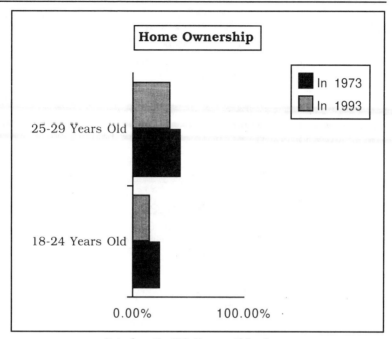

Data from the U.S. Bureau of the Census

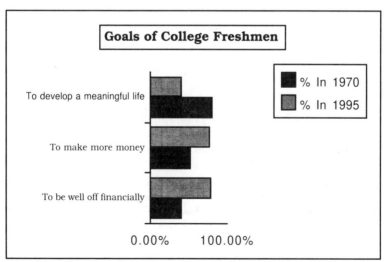

Data from the American Demographic Association
(Horizontal numbers indicate percentage feeling each is a major goal.)

95

5. The nature of "family" has changed for all ages, and this is particularly evident with young adults. There was a time when talking about a "young family" brought an image of a husband, a wife, two children, a dog, and a cat living together in a ranch style home. That isn't true today. The percentage of young adults who are married has gone down significantly:

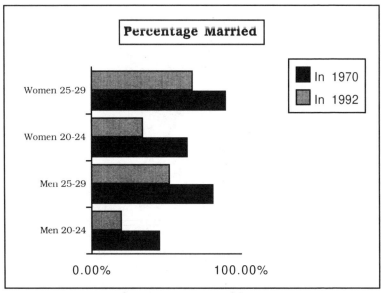

Data from the U.S. Bureau of the Census

The chart on the next page shows that the percentage of unmarried mothers has continued to increase. The overall percentage of single parents has risen not only because of unmarried mothers but also because of the divorce rate. Large numbers of today's young adults spent part of their childhood in single-parent homes, and some of those same persons are themselves now single parents.

When we talk about reaching out as congregations to young adults, we need to be thinking not only about married couples, both with children and without children, but also about young adult singles and single parents. Our churches need to learn how to be as welcoming to an unmarried mother and her child as to a newlywed couple.

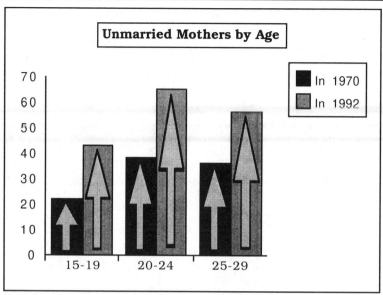

Data from the U.S. Bureau of the Census. Births per 1,000 unmarried women.
Unmarried women are defined as those not married at the time of the child's birth.

6. Young adults tend to view the church differently than older adults and are far more likely to be critical when the church seems like a bureaucracy. A study done in 1993 and replicated in 1994 asked young adults who were not church members, young adults who were church members, and older adults who were church members to share their impressions of the church as a bureaucracy and of the importance of being a church member. Some striking differences emerge:

Statement	19-35 Nonm.	19-35 Memb.	36 & Older Memb.
The local church is too much like an institution or a bureaucracy.	68%	61%	30%
You can be a good Christian even though you don't belong to a local church.	86%	73%	21%

*LifeQuest research results, 1993, 1994. Information previously cited in The Andrew Center publication **Fifty Ways to Reach Young Singles, Couples, & Families**.*

There are clearly differences between nineteen to thirty-five-year-olds who are not members of a church and those who are, but the most intriguing differences are between young adults who are church members and older adults who are church members. The differences are sufficiently great that it's not difficult to understand the existence of some tensions between younger adults and older adults in many congregations.

Many young adults who completed the survey commented that the decision-making structures of the local church are just too slow. Several young adults also feel that churches are too concerned with finances and need to show more concern for the spiritual life of members and for service to the community. When asked if they had shared these concerns within their local churches, the majority of those surveyed said they had not. One wrote: "I really like the older members of the church, and they've made me feel accepted. I don't want to offend them, which I would if I tried to explain why it drives me crazy to spend forty minutes in a meeting deciding whether to serve peanut butter sandwiches or cheese sandwiches to go along with the chili at an all-church supper. It took us five months to get approval to paint the room our class meets in. We volunteered to buy the paint and do the work, but it still had to go through all these approval stages by property, the trustees, and the board."

Older adult members, of course, also have their anxieties. One concerned member who was in his sixties wrote: "I know that a lot of our younger members don't like to be involved in the boards and committees. It feels to them like it takes too much time to accomplish anything, and they're probably right. But the church has almost four hundred members, and we don't have the right to just do what we want because we've been elected to a position. There are procedures to be followed."

A great many young adults are also not convinced that one must be a member of a local church in order to be a Christian. This is true not only for those who aren't involved in a church but also for many who are thoroughly involved. Older members of the church tend to view the local congregation as part of the body of Christ and cannot conceive of being a Christian in isolation. No doubt this difference in perspective has a lot to do with the lower numbers of young adults who actually join a local church.

Welcoming Young Adults

Obviously we can't erase the differences in life experience or in perspective between young adults and older adults. Most of the churches in North America have disproportionate numbers of older adults. If your church is one of those fortunate enough to be an exception, you are probably already doing several of the things suggested here. We especially recommend:

- **Helping older adults in the church better understand the perspective of young adults** both inside and outside of the church. Your involvement of church groups in a study of this book is one way to accomplish that. You may also want to study The Andrew Center report *Fifty Ways to Reach Young Singles Couples, and Families.* When possible, involve both young adults and older adults in the study process so that you have good interaction as you talk about the issues.

- **Implement as many of the suggestions as possible from the chapter on *Welcoming Children*.** Creating an atmosphere attractive to children is one of the best possible ways to create an atmosphere which is welcoming for their parents.

- **Help members of the congregation be sure that they are just as welcoming to young singles and to couples** who do not have children as they are to young couples with children. Young adult couples who do not yet have children are usually not appreciative of the suggestion that surely they'll be starting to have them soon! Even if your church doesn't have any young adult singles, it's still possible to warmly welcome singles who visit. Older members of the congregation sometimes "adopt" young adult singles, inviting into their homes for meals and taking an interest in their lives. When you've gotten a few visitors transformed to active participants, you have the core group for a young singles group. The same can be true for married couples without children.

- **Make a special effort to help older members understand the unique circumstances of single parents.** These persons are often very interested in spiritual issues and in what the church at its best can offer, but are quickly turned off by the implied disapproval of their unmarried or divorced status. Classes and groups designed to help people become more welcoming need to point out the importance of not immediately asking someone where his or her spouse is. There may not be a spouse!

- **Recognize the need for variety in worship services.** For some congregations this means starting a contemporary service. For others it means integrating more contemporary elements such as hymns and drama into an existing service. Help people understand the reasons for such changes, and continue interpreting those reasons. [For more help on this, see The Andrew Center book *Creating Quality in Ministry*, which includes substantial chapters on improving traditional worship and on starting contemporary worship.]

- **Be prepared to more quickly integrate enthusiastic young adults into the life of the church.** Don't wait until annual elections to invite people to serve on a board, commission, committee, or task force in which they are interested.

- **If your church is to be sensitive to the needs of young adults on a continuing basis, then you need to have persons of that age range as members of the major decision-making groups in your congregation.** That way their perspective is always available.

- **Recognize the reality that young adults who have not grown up in the church may not be familiar with many things which the rest of us take for granted.** Note again many of the recommendations shared in the chapters on *Experiencing Hospitality in the Church* and *Welcoming Strangers*.

- **Provide many opportunities for young adults and older adults to interact with one another.** Differences in perspective are not as important when people know and like one another. Some young adults reading this book will feel that they do not have the differences in perspective that are described. Where that is the case, it is very often because healthy interactions between young adults and older adults are a regular part of the life of the congregation.

Young Adults and Church Structure

As suggested earlier, young adults are often not as patient as older adults with the slow decision-making process which dominates many of our congregations. Sharing specific models for church organization goes beyond the scope of this book, but it is crucial to recognize that truly welcoming young adults generally means moving toward a less restrictive and more permission-giving kind of church organization.

There are large numbers of older adults in most congregations who would also like to see some changes in this direction. In a congregational survey of an established Midwestern congregation, people had some very strong words about the organizational structure in place at that time:

- "The organization is too top heavy – throw it all away and we'll find out what's important."

- "I think we could get the same results with many fewer organizational type meetings."

- "Our limited free time needs to be spent on what's really needed rather than on filling positions established years ago."

The main barrier to streamlining church organizational structures and decision-making processes is that it requires a greater degree of trust. People must be willing to trust others to make decisions and to be supportive of groups with which they are not personally involved. Large congregations are more likely to have such an atmosphere because of the impossibility of a significant percentage of the membership being involved in every decision. Smaller congregations which have functioned for years with systems that required broad agreement before any change was made may find it initially difficult to let decisions be made more rapidly and by fewer people. Failure to make that transition, however, can have a very limiting effect on church growth.

Growing churches are increasingly characterized by:

- A structure that emphasizes DOING more than DECIDING. There are fewer decision-making groups and more action groups.

- A structure with fewer standing committees and more task forces or mission groups appointed as needs arise.

- A greater willingness to trust individuals and groups to make decisions without having several layers of approval.

- A clearer separation of those decisions which have significant impact on the whole congregation and need the involvement of many persons from those decisions which affect only a few people or are of relatively minor importance.

And if you come upon the perfect organizational structure for your church which pleases persons of all ages, PLEASE send the details of the structure to the authors of this book! We'd love to have it. For the present, most of us are in transition, seeking to make improvements at the pace which our congregations can accept.

Hospitality and the Overlooked

Concept: The congregation which takes seriously a biblical understanding of hospitality does not place restrictions on its welcome and actively seeks out those whom others might overlook.

Clarence came from a long line of relatively uneducated people who had not attended church. He didn't have any particularly negative feelings about the church, but it had never seemed relevant to his life. When his sixteen-year-old son was caught selling drugs, however, Clarence felt like his own life was coming apart. The son faced a potentially stiff jail term, and the resulting stress affected the entire family. Clarence and his wife did not see the situation in the same way and reached the point that they couldn't even talk about it with each other.

Desperate for some kind of help or perspective, Clarence decided to go to church. He came a little late, just after the announcements and the prelude, and realized, as he slipped into a pew, that he wasn't dressed as well as the others who were present. Members of the congregation sang hymns, said prayers, and greeted one another at the appropriate times. One of the hymns was vaguely familiar to Clarence, but he didn't know the others. When greetings were exchanged, he received only a weak smile and handshake from a man seated next to him.

The Scripture reading was utterly incomprehensible, and the sermon seemed full of references Clarence didn't understand: "Now this is like the story of the prodigal son. . . ." (What story of the prodigal son? And what is a prodigal?) "The atonement of Christ. . . ." (Atonement?) "The grace of God was sufficient to see her through those difficult times. . . ." (Grace? Is that the name of a person God sent to help her?)

By the time the service ended, he felt certain that he had made one of the major mistakes of his life. Whatever made him think that he could feel at home in the church? What made him think that there would be a message of hope which he could understand?

The Gospel for All People

Churches generally succeed in growth because active members invite their friends, family members, coworkers, and neighbors to attend worship or other church events. That kind of growth is certainly consistent with an attitude of hospitality toward others, and it's only natural that the people we individually pull into the church are very often going to be those with whom we have already established relationships.

As discussed earlier in this book, however, that kind of growth tends to make for a church in which people are very much alike. Our friends, neighbors, and coworkers are generally persons who are very similar to us in at least some respects. They are generally persons of comparable income level, the same racial or ethnic background, and similar educational level. But what about those persons who are different from us in significant ways?

In **Luke 14:7-14**, Jesus describes the places of honor generally accorded others at a wedding banquet. Then our Lord suggests that those giving a lunch or dinner consider changing the guest list:

When you give a banquet, invite the poor, the crippled, the lame, and the blind. And you will be blessed because they cannot repay you, for you will be repaid at the resurrection of the righteous.
Luke 14:13-14

Chapter fourteen continues with Jesus telling the Parable of the Great Dinner in verses fifteen through twenty-four. In that

104

parable, the one who held a great banquet was disappointed by the many who gave excuses and did not come. As a result, "the poor, the crippled, the lame, and the blind were invited and then people were simply drawn from the street to finish filling the places for the banquet. Jesus challenges us to reach out with hospitality to those who would otherwise stay outside the circumference of our relationships and the life of the church.

If we take that parable and the Parable of the Good Samaritan seriously, then we will find ourselves reaching out to many persons we would have otherwise overlooked. The strongest congregations have always understood and practiced that concept.

George Miller lived near Elizabethtown, Pennsylvania, from 1722 through 1898. When one of his oxen was stolen, George did not sue the person responsible because he did not want the whipping required by British law to fall on the thief. His neighbors, however, had the thief arrested.

Miller then walked twenty miles to Lancaster, Pennsylvania, where the thief was detained, to provide him with warm bedding. He demonstrated hospitality toward the thief, treating him as a friend, while his neighbors perceived the thief as an enemy. This kind of outreach in the name of Christ transforms lives and embodies the kind of peace-making to which we have all been called. [*History of the Church of the Brethren – Eastern Pennsylvania* by S.R. Zug, pp. 511-512]

Another account from Pennsylvania comes from Clyde and Emma Weaver, friends of Fred Bernhard. Emma's grandparents, who lived in Lebanon County, Pennsylvania, responded to a man who came to their door seeking help on a cold winter evening. Practicing hospitality, they gave him a meal, lodging for the night, and breakfast the next morning. They did not know him, and many people would have felt they took a significant risk.

After breakfast, their guest told them that he had just arrived from Germany and had no money to pay them. They did not expect any pay and made that clear, but their guest still wished to show his appreciation. He offered them a recipe for seasoned meat which had been passed through his family for generations. The result of that recipe, which was not actually used in the Weaver family for many years, was what we know today as Lebanon Bologna, and it has become a popular dish in some parts of North America.

Jesse M. Burall, Fred's father-in-law, shared another account. When German POWs were incarcerated near Camp Detrick in Frederick, Maryland, the government decided to let them work during the day on area farms. Mr. Burall arranged for six of these workers, who automatically came with an armed guard.

The policy was for the prisoners to be fed lunch outside. Mr. Burall, however, insisted that the men eat at the table with the rest of the family. This practice continued over the two-year period from 1943 to 1945. Table hospitality and prayer were always shared, and genuine friendships developed. Mr. Burall's only regret was that he couldn't get the guard to join them at the table. "Then the circle would have been completed," he said. Such outreach provides healing of relationships and natural opportunities for sharing the faith.

Compare those perspectives with our tendency today to want harsher sentences for those charged with crimes, to lock our doors to strangers, and to avoid contact with persons who represent differing ideologies.

The Overlooked

As shared at the beginning of this book, hospitality is not optional and is also not safe. The historical examples of persons sharing hospitality which have just been given were not without risk, but people chose to act consistently with their understanding of the gospel. The authors of this book are not urging that people stop using common sense in terms of safety for themselves and others, but most of us pass up numerous opportunities to build friendships with persons who are different from us. Some of those we overlook may truly live next door to the church!

Many churches are located in neighborhoods which have residents who differ in significant ways from the persons in the congregation. This is increasingly true in North America as vast numbers of persons each Sunday morning drive past many other churches to worship and learn in the church of their choice. Steve Clapp has repeatedly encountered such realities in the process of helping local congregations with surveys and profiles of their membership and their ministry situations.

The chart which follows compares strength of agreement with two statements by members of an urban congregation with the average in other North American churches and with the average among growing congregations. The two statements were:

• Members of this church are similar in values and lifestyle to people who live immediately around the church.

• Our church is very involved with the community around the church.

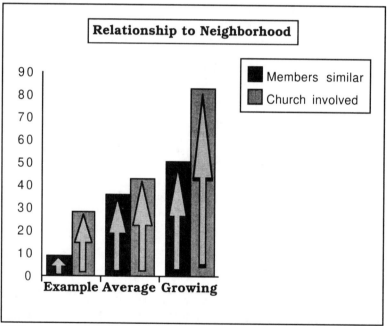

LifeQuest provided chart. Bars show the percentage agreeing or strongly agreeing with each statement.

In this particular urban congregation, fewer than 10% of the persons completing the survey felt that their members were similar in values and lifestyle to those living near the church. Fewer than 30% felt that their congregation was involved in the community around the church. There were significant racial, educational, and economic differences between church members and the neighborhood.

Those differences had begun to make members of the church feel uncomfortable coming to the church building for evening meetings and also reluctant to invite their friends to church. People in the church knew almost no one in the neighborhood. While this example represents a more extreme situation than many, it is far from unique. What would it mean for the church to move from locked doors and fearful scheduling of activities to a spirit of hospitality toward the community around the church? It might mean:

- Door-to-door canvassing by couples from the church to share information with people in the neighborhood about the church and to learn more about the people in that area.

- Providing a free ice cream social for the neighborhood and encouraging all active congregational members to share in serving and visiting.

- Surveying the neighborhood to find out what programs are needed and opening the church as appropriate to help with support groups, recreation, or other areas of need.

- Actively inviting people in the neighborhood to attend other church activities, including worship services.

The majority of the persons who are overlooked by members of most congregations, of course, are not necessarily those in the neighborhood around the church facilities. The church should extend hospitality to all who come, including those described on the following pages. Before deciding to intentionally reach out to a particular category of persons, it's important to evaluate the extent to which the congregation as a whole is prepared to embrace those individuals. Where anxiety or fear is associated with a particular category, it may be necessary to address those feelings before taking congregational initiative to invite such persons to the church. Ignoring those feelings may do harm to both members and guests. When such persons appear at church through their own initiative or that of others, we are of course challenged to put aside our fears and follow Christ's welcoming example. Some of those who are likely to be overlooked include:

- People whose educational level is above or below that of most in the congregation. Educational differences, similarly to financial differences, sometimes form a solid barrier to friendships. As we think about our relationships with others, we should be careful that we do not permit the fact that another person has either more or less education than ourselves to keep us from extending hospitality in the name of Christ.

- People whose economic and/or social status differs from that of most in the congregation. How many patients with no college education have considered inviting their physician to church? How many professionals have considered inviting a custodian to church? If we take the biblical concept of hospitality seriously, those differences should not keep us from extending an invitation to be part of what is valuable to us — the church.

- People who have problems with alcoholism or other forms of drug addiction. While some churches readily open their buildings for meetings by A.A. groups, most of us do not often think about inviting persons dealing with such difficulties to be part of the life of the church. Those persons, however, can gain a great deal from the Christian community; and they also have rich gifts to offer us because of what they are overcoming.

- People who have been in trouble with the law and the families of those persons. The opening example of this chapter described a father affected by his son's arrest and potential imprisonment. An earlier chapter talked about the experiences of a released convict named Eddie. Our communities have ever-increasing numbers of persons who have had such experiences and who need the hospitality of Christian people.

- Victims of crime. A couple in their mid-fifties were crushed, angered, and then perplexed by the unsolved murder of their married daughter, who had been in her mid-twenties at the time of her murder near the entrance to her home. The surrounding questions and grief caused her parents to be understandably fixated on the reasons for her death and the identity of her murderer. The police explanation of "probable random violence" was not satisfactory to them. Do we let our discomfort and lack of certainty about what to say keep us from inviting and welcoming such persons?

- Unmarried persons who are living together. As shared in the chapter on young adults, increasing numbers of people fall into this category. Such persons can benefit greatly from both Christ's unconditional love and his invitation to discipleship. Included in the Christian community, they have opportunity to discover a personal ethic that teaches God's boundaries and call to accountability in covenantal relationships expressed in marriage.

- Persons of different sexual orientation. The inclusion of this category is undoubtedly disconcerting to some. It is best understood in the spirit of Christ's invitation to come "just as we are"; Christ–like love is compassion-ate and hospitable. However – as we noted in an earlier chapter – welcoming persons is not synonymous with accepting all aspects of their lifestyle or behavior. It is important to link the act of hospitality with the call to discipleship. Ultimately, we welcome the outsider to walk with us on the road of Christian obedience and faithfulness.

- Persons of other races or ethnic backgrounds. These individuals are very often missing from our congre-gations and also from our circles of friends. Tensions in public schools are frequently along racial lines. Those of us in the Christian community should be taking the initiative to extend hospitality to persons whose skin color or ancestry differs from our own.

- Persons who are physically or mentally-challenged. They not normally present in significant numbers in our congregations. Some of our churches have not eliminated the architectural barriers to persons with various physical disabilities. It's difficult to offer hospitality with our words when our physical facilities convey something entirely different. Those who are mentally-challenged may require significant adjustments by the rest of us, but their presence will generally enrich our lives. If few churches in your area are offering programs for the mentally-challenged, then this could be an area for significant growth in your church. We should offer hospitality to the physically and mentally challenged, not only for their sake and because of the spirit of hospitality, but also because we have so much to learn from persons who have carried such burdens.

- Persons who are in the military. These individuals may be overlooked by those in peace church traditions. Persons who are opposed to military service may be overlooked by those congregations which encourage patriotism and military service. Our welcome needs to extend to persons in both categories, recognizing that Christ expects us to extend the welcome and also that we can gain from the perspective of those who differ from us.

Obviously the listing could be extended for many additional pages. We refer those wanting to know more on this topic to helpful chapters in Steve Clapp and Sam Detwiler's book **Sharing Living Water** and to the coming Andrew Center publication **Ministry with the Forgotten**.

Remember that many of the categories shared in this chapter bring us into connection with persons who may make us feel uncomfortable or with whom we may have serious disagreements. The essence of hospitality, however, focuses on the obligations of the host rather than those of the guest.

Centuries ago the Benedictines began practicing biblical hospitality to strangers without knowing or caring about the background of those persons. Monasteries were situated in towns and the country as common places where hospitality could be found. The Rule of St. Benedict was given sometime between 530 and 543 A.D. and is still known and practiced:

111

> *Let all the guests that come be received like Christ*
> *himself, for he will say: "I was a stranger and ye*
> *took me in"* [*Commentary on the Rule of St. Benedict*
> by Paul Delatte, p. 330].

These guests were considered so important that the Superior was even ordered to break his fast for the sake of the guest, unless it was a principal fast day.

The guests represented Christ, so the monks did all that they could to see that each person was treated as though Christ were present in that individual. They provided for both the temporal and spiritual needs of guests. Such a standard would greatly increase our personal welcomes to the strangers we encounter and also the welcome of our congregations to those who are too often overlooked.

How Welcoming are
Your Physical Facilities?

Concept: The church's physical facilities can be part of your congregation's welcome or can be a barrier to participation by members and visitors.

"I sure feel ashamed of myself for all the times I said we didn't need a wheelchair ramp or an elevator," Howard gasped to his wife as he used the railing to help pull himself up the steps from the church basement to the main floor.

"Don't you think you should rest a few minutes before going the rest of the way?" his wife Martha asked.

"Can't risk the loss of momentum. I'll be okay," but his voice didn't sound reassuring to himself or to Martha. Since a triple-bypass surgery nine months earlier, Howard continued to feel like everything took three times as much energy as it should. The surgeon had told him that it would take six months for him to resume normal activity, but Howard felt more like it would be six years, if ever.

"I still think we should ask them to move the class to one of the first floor rooms," Martha said as she took Howard's arm to offer him some support. He didn't jerk his arm away from her and make his frequent snorting noise, which told her that he was indeed feeling drained.

"But there really isn't another classroom upstairs that's available. What would they do, make the Happy Days class change to the basement? Those people are older than I am. I think you have to have arthritis, diabetes, or heart disease to be a member of the class."

"Howard," Martha scolded, "you know better than to talk that way."

He sighed as he paused for a moment a third of the way from the top of the stairs. "I sure do," he agreed. "The truth of the matter is that most of the people in that class are in better shape than I am. Maybe we should ask them to trade rooms."

While Howard and Martha were making their way up the stairs, Paul and Jane, a very healthy young adult couple, were getting ready to visit another congregation on the opposite side of town. They were driving around First Church's block for the third time. "I really think it's okay to park in the restaurant's lot," Jane offered to her husband for the second time. "The restaurant looks like it's closed and there are a few cars there already. Those must be people going to church."

"But if you're wrong, they're going to tow the car. That sign looks pretty explicit and doesn't say that Sunday is an exception," her husband Paul responded. "We saw a lot of people parking a couple of blocks down the street and walking. I think that's what people do when the lot by the church gets full."

"We could just keep driving around the block for another hour or so," Jane suggested, "and then the service would be over."

Paul laughed at her comment and at himself. "You're right," he admitted as he pulled into the restaurant's parking lot. "We're going to need time anyway to figure out which door to go in. There must be five entrances, and we've seen people use all of them except the big doors that look like they'd lead to the sanctuary."

"But I think that's just like my home church," said Jane. "Because there's no parking right in front of the sanctuary, no one ever enters that way. Sometimes they even forget to unlock those doors."

"Well, this church is even bigger than yours. We'll be lost for sure if we go in the wrong door." They got out of their car and headed toward the church.

In another church in the same community, Betty and Sarah were visiting with each other as they washed their hands in the women's restroom. Sarah and Betty were both single parents who worked for the same company. Sarah had belonged to the congregation for seven years, and Betty was there as Sarah's guest. Betty didn't have a church home and had talked with Sarah after work about feeling an emptiness in her life. Sarah had suggested that Betty and her young child attend church that weekend.

Betty, however, already had a couple of concerns, which she began expressing as she pulled paper towels out of the dispenser. "Sarah, has the paint around the baseboard in here been peeling for a long time?"

"Peeling?" Sarah looked at the baseboard. "It is peeling, isn't it? The truth is that I don't think I've ever noticed before. It probably hasn't been peeling for too long."

"I don't want to make a big deal out of it," Betty said as her face flushed slightly. "It's just that it would make me nervous to have Kimberly in here with us. It seems to me that my child will put anything that fits into her mouth. It would be just like her to chew on that paint because the color is neat."

"Yuck!" Sarah made a face. "That doesn't help us make a good impression, does it?"

"I don't mean that I'm rejecting your church because some paint is peeling," Betty said. "It's just that the peeling paint on top of how crowded the nursery room looked made me wonder if your church has been able to handle the fast growth it's been experiencing."

Underestimating the Message of the Facilities

We can too easily grow comfortable with aspects of our physical facilities that really aren't welcoming. Betty noticed the peeling paint in the restroom right away and was concerned about it as a potential hazard to children, but Sarah had not noticed it. In that particular congregation, the paint had in fact been peeling for about two years. Our physical facilities do communicate a message to members and visitors. We want that message to be consistent with what we are attempting to communicate through our words to people.

Lack of attention to physical facilities can especially be a problem for those of us in traditions which emphasize simple lifestyles and who don't want to go overboard in what we spend on the building and grounds. Think about the barriers or potential barriers experienced by the persons at the beginning of this chapter:

- Stairs and steep inclines can be significant problems for persons in wheelchairs, for persons with arthritis, and for persons with conditions such as heart disease, emphysema, and severe asthma.

- Unclear parking instructions can leave people in a state of confusion. The restaurant parking lot near First Church was in fact available to church members and visitors on Sunday mornings and also on weekday evenings, but the sign didn't say so. An arrangement with the restaurant to include a sign about Sunday and evening parking would have ended some confusion. A system of parking ushers or greeters can also provide a means to help people deal with limited parking – or simply to help them feel at home when they arrive.

- Not knowing which door to use for a church can be frustrating to those who have not attended before. Churches which have multiple entrances need to have signs which make it clear which entrances are for the sanctuary, for education, and for church offices.

- Betty had the impression that the nursery in Sarah's church was crowded. While a church which feels comfortably full and busy can convey a sense of enthusiasm and energy, no one wants to feel confined. And a crowded nursery is a little disturbing! People also do not want to be forced into too close a proximity to other persons during worship, classes, or fellowship times. People are reluctant to linger and visit if the narthex area of the sanctuary is always jammed.

- Although people often do not think to verbalize that the church's physical facilities appear well–maintained, that in fact is an expectation which almost everyone has. People don't want to see peeling paint where children might eat it, as was the case in Sarah's church. They also don't want to see peeling paint on the outside of the church or in any other place. They don't want to find cracks in the sidewalks or the stairs which are big enough to be dangerous. They also expect the church grounds to be clean, well–trimmed, and attractive.

The church is not a building. We know that. But one or more buildings house the majority of our church services and programs. The welcome communicated by those facilities needs to be just as positive as that communicated by the words of the pastor, other church staff, and members.

A Checklist on Physical Facilities

Check as many of the following statements as apply to the physical facilities of your congregation. Items which you check merit further evaluation by appropriate groups in the congregation.

___ **Our sanctuary seats far more people than our average worship attendance.** While people don't want to be crowded, they also feel strange if sitting too far away from other worshipers. They are not likely to greet or to be greeted by persons not sitting near them. If your sanctuary seems to be swallowing your congregation, encourage people to sit more toward the front of the sanctuary or to consider meeting in another part of the church. A change of location works especially well for a contemporary service.

___ **Our sanctuary is 80% or more full at most worship services.** If that's the case, then you may be getting close to a leveling off of worship attendance. People in general seem reluctant to sit in a sanctuary that is completely full. You may need to consider expanded physical facilities or a move to an additional service of worship.

___ **Our sanctuary doesn't provide an especially**

attractive setting for worship. This generally means there's nothing wrong with the sanctuary but also nothing unique or uplifting about it. Unless you are part of a religious tradition which places great emphasis on simplicity in worship, you may wish to consider what might be done to increase the beauty and warmth of the sanctuary. That could include new altar and pulpit coverings (paraments) if appropriate to your tradition, stained glass windows, new pews, refinishing existing pews, repainting, or other improvements. Remember, as in one's own home, it isn't always the amount of money spent on furnishings so much as the feeling of warmth conveyed by the colors and textures which are present. Persons with background in interior design can often be a significant help even if they are not experienced in church interiors.

___ **Our sanctuary and other facilities aren't especially "child friendly."** If children spill something on a pew, chair, or the floor, does it create a significant problem? If so, as opportunities arise, try to increase the comfort level for children and their parents. Use stain resistant fabrics wherever possible.

___ **Altar furnishings in our sanctuary cannot be arranged to accommodate drama or other innovations in worship.** If this is the case, then you must work under some limitations if you want to experiment with more contemporary forms of worship. There may be limitations on what can be done about this unless the altar furnishings are showing age and replacement would be logical. If your church decides to start a separate contemporary service, then one option may be to hold that service in another part of the church building. Some congregations which have sanctuaries which are much larger than needed for the average worship attendance have taken out a few pews or rows of chairs near the front to make more flexible space available.

___ **The speaker system in our sanctuary doesn't work well, and a hearing-impaired person would have problems knowing what is happening.** If that's the case, then you should investigate upgrading that system. People develop hearing problems for a number of reasons but are especially likely to experience difficulties with advancing age. Given the increasing percentage of the population in North America which is over the age of sixty-five, needs in this area will continue to increase. Our worship settings should be ones in which persons with impaired hearing feel comfortable. That generally means a good speaker system and special units for those who need extra enhancement. Deaf persons, of course, can benefit from signing; and increasing numbers of congregations are making that available.

____ **We couldn't add classes or groups without expanding our Christian education facilities.** If that is the case, then it's time to take a careful look at available space. Classes and small groups are among the very best ways to help new persons feel welcomed into the life of the congregation and to give those persons opportunity to build relationships with others. It's often easier to accomplish growth by adding class and group opportunities than by trying to increase the numbers in existing groups. Dividing some existing rooms, experimenting with additional times for classes or groups, and other strategies may be alternatives to construction. At a certain point, however, building more space may be absolutely critical.

____ **Our Christian education classrooms can't really be described as comfortable and attractive.** If they aren't, then do something about it! They are part of the welcome of your church to present members and to potential members. Some churches spend enormous amounts of money on attractive worship settings but almost completely neglect Christian education facilities. Rooms need to feel bright, warm, and welcoming. Chairs need to be comfortable and of appropriate size for the age level. Carpeting can be a pleasant touch in any classroom but should be stain resistant.

____ **We do not have a comfortable and attractive area for youth to meet.** If that's the case, then you need to involve the young people themselves in the process of upgrading one or more meeting areas. Remember that what is comfortable and welcoming to teenagers may not always be what adults would choose! Many youth, for example, appreciate having an entire wall which is painted white and on which people can feel free to write, draw, or paint whatever they want. A good sound system linked to a CD player, television, and VCR can be a significant help with programming and also an asset for recreational times. Consider having a small area for food preparation where the youth meet to save extra movement and also to eliminate the problem of needing to leave the church kitchen absolutely spotless in order to avoid getting in trouble!

___ **We do not have all the ramps, elevators, and/or other accommodations needed for persons with physical handicaps and other mobility or energy limitations to use our facilities.** Making these changes can be an expensive process, and some churches are tempted not to do so on the basis that "No one who needs a ramp or elevator is coming to our church right now." As discussed in the chapter *Hospitality and the Overlooked*, such persons are also not likely to start coming unless the accommodations to their needs have been met. There's nothing more unwelcoming than discovering that you can't even get inside a building without the help of one or more other persons. Even if your congregation lacks persons who are restricted to wheelchairs or crutches, you almost certainly have people who suffer from other conditions who can benefit from a reduction in the number of stairs with which they must cope.

___ **We need more parking for our congregation.** If so, start developing a strategy for expanding your current parking. That could include asking a nearby business for permission to use its lot when the business is closed and offering to pay for a sign to that effect. It could include utilizing parking ushers or greeters to watch for people who need help finding a parking space. It could include acquiring more property for an expanded or additional parking lot. Hospitality includes not expecting people to walk too far in order to attend church events. Having to park five blocks away isn't reasonable.

___ **We have plenty of parking, but it isn't paved. We simply park in a dirt or grass lot adjacent to the church.** If that's the case, then you need to consider paving that lot. When it rains, people get their shoes covered with mud if they have to walk through a grass or dirt parking lot. That doesn't make people feel they've been warmly welcomed by the congregation. A family visiting a congregation in eastern Pennsylvania returned from the worship service to discover that their car had sunk a couple of inches into the grass-covered lot following a heavy rain. The husband and teenage son both became covered with mud as they pushed the car free. Though they laughed about the incident at the time, they did not return to that congregation.

___ **The narthex area or entrance to the sanctuary is**

fairly small and doesn't encourage visiting by those who come. If this is the case, give careful study to strategies for improvement, including the possible elimination of some pews at the back of the sanctuary or an expansion by construction. The time just before and just after a worship service is a prime opportunity for people to visit with one another. You want a physical setting which encourages those interchanges to take place. Churches which are arranged so that their coffee or fellowship time can be held in the narthex or adjacent to it have larger percentages of individuals stay for that time and mix with one another as a result.

___ Our church office facilities feel crowded and/or aren't especially attractive. The church office is the setting in which many persons experience the hospitality of the church. If the office is too small and feels crowded, people feel uncomfortable and won't stay long. While it may sometimes feel desirable to a busy church secretary or pastor to have people stay only briefly, that isn't the overall impression which the church wants to give.

Some churches provide comfortable chairs or a small lounge area just outside the office so that people can wait comfortably to see the pastor without necessarily being engaged in a lengthy conversation with a secretary who is trying desperately to complete the newsletter or bulletin! The office of the pastor or of any other professional staff member should be attractive and comfortable. You want that space to create a warm, safe feeling which will encourage people to be open and honest in their sharing.

You also want the office to include well-maintained, current equipment to help the secretary, pastor, and any other staff members do their work efficiently and comfortably. Equipment which produces sloppy-looking newsletters and bulletins conveys to people that the church doesn't take these matters seriously. Attractive materials convey the hospitality of the congregation.

___ It's actually a little difficult to find our church if one isn't familiar with the community. If this is the case, then you need to invest in signs which can help people locate your building. In fact, you need signs showing the way to your church even if it is easy to find! You also need a sign on the church building or in front of the church building which clearly identifies it! Some churches simply assume that everyone will know their name without the necessity of its appearing prominently on the building itself. That's not the kind of welcoming spirit the church wants to convey.

___ **Our church building(s) and grounds don't stand out as especially attractive or inviting.** If that's the case, then it's time for work to be done! The building needs to communicate that the body of Christ takes pride in the place where it gathers and welcomes others who wish to share in its activities.

The preceding checklist, of course, is not exhaustive. We do hope it will encourage you to think with greater intentionality about what is communicated by your church building(s) and grounds. Just as our residences communicate something of our values and personalities, so also do our church buildings convey a sense of the values and personality of the congregation. Be sure the message is one of welcome!

The Changing Shape
Of Worship and Program

Concept: We should continually strive to make
the services and programs of the church expressions
of the welcome we want extended to all people.

As the increasing pace of change affects every aspect of
society, we can't escape continually examining the routines,
procedures, and practices which are part of the Christian
community. The church which takes seriously the provision of
hospitality to its members and to visitors will stay alert for ways
to further widen the welcome which it offers. In this chapter we
share some further possibilities which may be helpful in your
congregation's outreach.

Creating Comfort in Worship

As soon as the organ began, Maxine realized that she had
misread the hymn number in the bulletin. She was on 588, but
it didn't appear that anyone else was. She had to get very close
to the man on her right in order to see what hymn number had
been chosen. 533. The threes had appeared as eights to her.
Why did the bulletin have to be in such small type? Even with
trifocals, she just couldn't make sense of letters and numbers in
small print.

And Maxine is hardly alone. Many people, of various ages,
have difficulty reading small print. Even books like this one, for
reasons of economy, tend to be printed in a smaller typeface
than is comfortable reading for many people. When printing
thousands of copies of a book, a difference in type size can make
a significant difference in the cost of the finished product. That's

not normally the case with bulletins for Sunday morning. Even if larger sheets of paper must be used to accommodate a larger type size in the bulletin, the additional cost is not high compared to the benefits it brings to many people. Some churches provide special large print bulletins for those with difficulty seeing, but that solution has two problems. First, it doesn't benefit visitors who often have no idea that the larger size is available. Second, it makes people feel self-conscious about their vision problems. If the print is larger and bolder for everyone, no one has to feel singled out.

Everything about the bulletin should be prepared with the visitor in mind. For example:

- The bulletin itself should extend a prominent welcome to visitors. It should be clear that guests are expected!

- If the bulletin contains something like a *Doxology* or the *Gloria Patri*, a hymn number or the words should be provided. Visitors should not be expected to be familiar with such traditions.

- If the Lord's Prayer is used, then people should at least be informed whether sins, debts, or trespasses is the wording used. A simple parenthesis after "The Lord's Prayer" indication in the bulletin can provide the word. Some congregations choose to print out the full wording to the prayer.

- No steps or responses should be taken for granted. The bulletin should include all the information needed for the service.

- Special instructions such as whether or not visitors can share in communion should be included in the bulletin.

Pastors and other worship leaders likewise want to continually keep the guest in mind in directing the service, being careful not to make assumptions. As pointed out in the checklist in the chapter *Welcoming Strangers*, those who share announcements and joys and concerns should be sure to introduce themselves and to speak in such a way that visitors will not feel excluded. Announcements which pertain to only a few people should generally not be made during the worship service.

Many pastors have learned that giving a brief introduction to a passage of Scripture often helps not only guests but also long-time members gain more from the biblical reading. Pastors who are sensitive to guests are careful to preach in a way that avoids theological jargon which may be unfamiliar to persons who have not been previously active in the life of a church.

The development of a theology of worship goes considerably beyond the scope of this book and the space available for this chapter. It is important, however, to stay aware of the tremendous diversity people feel about what constitutes meaningful worship. Traditional hymns and organ music are on target for large numbers of persons who have been raised in the church, but there are growing numbers of people who appreciate more contemporary forms of music. Some churches have substantial numbers of people who like country western and even Christian rock. Contemporary Christian hymns, such as those by Michael W. Smith, have gained significant acceptance in many congregations. Practicing hospitality means having appreciation for the wide range of what speaks to people and enables their ability to offer meaningful worship to God. The following statements came out of a single congregation of 137 people:

- "I liked it on Youth Sunday when some of the young people played CDs and tapes of songs they especially liked. I thought one of the songs by Tori Amos was wonderful."

- "I can't believe the pastor let the teenagers play some of that music in worship. That song by Tori Amos was the limit for me. Why can't we all agree on some of the great music by people like Charles Wesley and Fannie Crosby?"

- "I listen to country western music all the time in the car. Why can't we have some music in church that's similar? The classical music and the organ may speak to some people, but the words don't mean a thing to me and the organ grates on my ear."

125

- "I have tried, but I simply cannot understand the fascination with contemporary Christian music. Our choir and some of the soloists keep doing things by Sandi Patti. But have they paid any attention to the words? All that music seems so shallow to me."

- "I find so much meaning in some of the music of Sandi Patti that we've been doing. She went through some hard times a few years ago, and it changed what she sings, or at least I think so."

- "We are so fortunate to have a good organ and such a skilled organist. I keep sitting in the sanctuary to listen to the postlude. She plays a lot of Bach, and those works lift my spirits and give me energy."

- "I can appreciate some of the more contemporary hymns and anthems we've been using, but I have to admit that the traditional songs are the ones which speak to me at the deepest levels. We have to include both kinds in the service."

We could keep providing quotes from that congregation, but you can already see the trend – diversity in what gives meaning to people!

Of course that's just talking about music, not about other aspects of worship, such as the use of drama or video instead of a sermon as discussed in earlier chapters. It seems increasingly impossible to have "a" service which will appeal to all age groups and interests. Some pastors feel like the only place they have achieved unity in worship is in uniting people in their conclusion that their needs are not being met!

Looking at worship through the lens of hospitality, however, should change our perspective. In terms of hospitality, our focus is not simply or even primarily on meeting our own needs. We want to meet the needs of others and especially of those who are strangers to us! We are the hosts and want the service to be meaningful to our guests.

That kind of switch in attitude can move a congregation in two different directions, depending on the size and resources of the church:

1. Churches which focus on hospitality find a greater acceptance of diversity within existing services of worship, with people recognizing that the needs of others should be met – and especially the needs of those who are guests and who may have been turned off by past experiences with worship.

2. Churches which focus on hospitality and have the needed resources in leadership, settings, and membership may create different types of services. Many will have a traditional service and a contemporary service. Some may choose to offer even greater variety such as: a small communion service, a traditional service, a contemporary service led by youth, and a service with gospel and country western music.

Offering variety in the services serves existing members by letting them select the style which speaks most effectively to them. The variety also serves prospective members, our guests, by giving them the opportunity to experience more than a single style of worship. The nontraditional opportunities are especially valuable to those persons who did not grow up in the church and thus have no substantial past history of a traditional style of worship.

We sometimes forget that there are different benefits to worship services which are relatively small in number and to those which are relatively large. In fact, some very large churches have chosen to create worship experiences which are likely to draw relatively small attendance because of the timing or location of the service. That might include an early morning service or a service in a small chapel rather than the sanctuary.

There are persons in our society who are very uncomfortable in large groups. Those persons will often find a service with an average attendance in the range of thirty to eighty more attractive than one with an average attendance in the hundreds. There are fewer persons with whom they need to interact, and the setting feels less threatening.

127

Of course worshiping with a small group, especially with as few as twenty or thirty people, may be quite uncomfortable for others. Some persons truly like to become lost in the crowd! They fear being put on the spot and would prefer slipping into the service and then slipping out. While we need to take steps to be sure we eventually become acquainted with such persons, we also need to respect their desire for a greater amount of privacy than we ourselves may feel.

Every congregation has limitations on the options which can be offered either in a single worship service or in multiple services. Looking at worship from the standpoint of hospitality, however, should enable us to focus more on the needs of others and less on our own needs. That doesn't mean that our own needs shouldn't be met in the service, but it does mean that we have the ability and desire to take a broader look, to care about meeting the needs of others.

A Caution

Having talked about the differences in our view of worship which come when we are concerned about the needs of our guests, one caution needs to be shared. **Worship is above all the offering which we make to God and the celebration of God's love.** In the worship setting, as in other settings in the church, we keep before us the need to show hospitality to others; but God is the ultimate focus.

We don't want to become so obsessed with offering endless variety to meet the needs of ourselves and others that we fail to recognize that our creator is the object of our worship. We don't want to make our own needs or the needs of others into idols which we worship instead of God. That's not an argument against diversity in worship. In fact seeing God as the focus of worship is actually liberating, for God clearly can and does accept worship in a multitude of forms. The danger is that we can let the forms become the object of worship rather than the means of worship.

In *The Screwtape Letters*, C.S. Lewis, writing fictional words of advice from the demon Screwtape to his nephew Wormwood, points out that the devil's needs can be met well by encouraging people to keep evaluating churches and searching for the ideal setting:

> *Surely you know that if a man can't be cured of*
> *churchgoing, the next best thing is to send him*
> *all over the city looking for the church that "suits"*
> *him until he becomes a taster or connoisseur*
> *of churches. . . . The search for a "suitable" church*
> *makes the man a critic where the Enemy wants*
> *him to be a pupil* [Tarrytown, NY; Spire Books
> edition © 1976, p. 81].

The "enemy" from the perspective of the demon is, of course, God. If sending people on a search for a "suitable" church is one of the strategies of contemporary demons, it is a strategy which has been successful in many ways! More and more people who move into a new community do shop for the church which feels best relative to their needs. Decreases in denominational loyalty over the last two decades have fueled the church-shopping mentality.

The purpose of greater variety in worship which we are advocating in this book isn't primarily to make our congregations competitive in a church-shopping market. The purpose is to make our congregations more genuinely welcoming by showing concern for the outward forms which will best enable people to connect with Jesus Christ. The result may be beneficial to us in terms of competition with other congregations, but that is not the purpose of the changes. The distinction seems to us an important one.

Baptism and Church Membership

In the spirit of hospitality, we need to be aware that our traditional style of public baptism and statement of membership vows in front of the entire congregation may pose a barrier for some persons. These are likely to be individuals who are not comfortable with large groups of people. This is especially the case for those denominational traditions which baptize only by immersion. Some people are terrified to be baptized by immersion in front of a large gathering. This is not an issue of their commitment to Christ or to the church but rather of their own mental health and well-being.

Some churches find it theologically impossible to handle baptism and member confirmation in any setting other than the regular congregational worship services. If that is one's position, obviously innovation in this area is not an option. If your theological perspective, however, gives room for a recognition of the psychological barriers which are present for a minority of people, there are some alternatives.

Consider the option of a semi-private baptism and/or confirmation service during the week or on a Sunday afternoon with immediate family, a deacon (if appropriate in your tradition), a board representative, and the pastor present. Public recognition can be given the following Sunday as people are introduced to the congregation and given membership materials either by their coming to the front of the church or by their standing briefly in the congregation. That kind of public acknowledgment is far less threatening to some persons than public baptism and repetition of vows.

Another alternative is to offer the semi-private service either right before or right after regular congregational worship. Some churches like to do so right after worship because that gives the opportunity for those who are moved to a decision during the worship service to make an immediate response.

Complex theological views and local church traditions clearly impact what can be done in this area. Our encouragement to you is to reflect on what it means to offer hospitality to those whose emotional well-being affects their comfort in public settings.

Prayer and Prayer Rooms

Like most congregations, the Oakland Church recognized that it could benefit from a great deal more prayer and a great deal less gossip! In reflecting on ways to encourage more prayer among those who were members and also seeking ways to respond to visitors who might find themselves especially moved, the church decided to establish a prayer room.

The prayer room offers comfortable furniture, warm lighting, and reading material about the spiritual life. At the end of each worship service, those who wish are invited to go to the prayer room, located near the sanctuary, where volunteers are present. The volunteers are there to answer questions and respond to the needs of those who come. This provides a setting for persons who feel a need for personal sharing or further prayer at the end of worship. This can include people who are ready to profess their faith in Christ, people who are dealing with the serious illness of a loved one, and people who find themselves with unanswered questions at the end of the service.

The prayer room also finds use during the week as people enter it to pray privately and to examine the resources which are found there. People have a hunger for prayer and for an overall deepening of the spiritual life, and the presence of the prayer room has become an outward sign of the importance of the spiritual life to the congregation. It in no way is a substitute for the kind of sharing and growing which occurs in organized classes and groups, but it is a response to the deep-seated need for personal prayer which exists in all of us.

Listening as Vital to Hospitality and Program

"To be perfectly candid," Helen shared with Beth, "I've been looking for a church which has a good group for single parents. I liked worshiping at your church last week, and I'm enjoying our lunch – but I feel the need to be part of a group of single parents rather than trying to fit in with a class filled with married couples or one with singles who have no children." Beth had met Helen the previous Sunday and had invited her to share lunch on Tuesday. The conversation about the church had been positive, but here was a significant need that the church wasn't meeting.

"I can sure understand that," replied Beth. "As I shared earlier, I was a single parent for almost four years. A group like that would have been a big help to me then. Actually we have at least three or four single parents in the church right now. What I wonder is if we couldn't get a group like that started."

"That sounds good, but I feel like I need a group now rather than a year from now. Some of us talked about a singles group in the church I was in before moving here, but the idea rusted on the agenda of the board."

"I understand, but it doesn't take us a year to start something new in our church. Our pastor and the board actively encourage people to do things to improve the church and its opportunities for people. Would you be willing to help start a new group?"

"Sure, but I'm brand new. Would people pay any attention to me?"

"Yes, they would. New people sometimes have the best ideas and the greatest enthusiasm. Tom Evans, the chairperson of our board, just joined the church two years ago. I'd also be glad to help get something started. If we talk to Pastor Jim and to Tom, they'll have more ideas on how to make something happen. We may already have more single parents than I know about, and there have to be others near the church. Why don't we see what's possible?"

They did. The result was not only that Helen joined the church but also that a single parents group started meeting before she had even transferred her membership. That was a congregation which took hospitality seriously and also believed in enabling ministries to happen.

Helen and Beth are part of a church on the east coast, but their experience could have happened at the Oakland Church. The Oakland Church's focus on hospitality has resulted in a greatly increased emphasis on listening to the needs of people – those already in the church and those interested in the church. The prayer room was a direct outgrowth of that listening.

Much church programming in the past at Oakland, as in many other congregations, has consisted of a few leaders identifying an area for emphasis and then "selling" the idea to the congregation. Such an approach can have good results if the programs are on target with the needs of many in the church, but people rarely have the enthusiasm for the ideas of others that they have for their own ideas!

Dynamic churches today increasingly have programs and opportunities generated by persons in the congregation, based on the needs, interests, and gifts of those persons. Such churches extend to people considerable freedom to move ahead with new program ideas. That may happen through the creation of a mission group or task force rather through an existing commission or committee.

Congregations need to be guided by an overall vision and mission. The vision and mission, however, need to be broad enough that the respective callings which people experience can become part of it. The new people which become part of the church, like Helen, may be the ones who start important new ministries.

The way that programming happens in churches around the country is being transformed. An understanding of hospitality can enrich the existing programs of your congregation and also result in significant new opportunities.

What Next?

Reflect again on the definition of hospitality which was shared in the first chapter of this book:

> **Hospitality** is the **attitude** and **practice** of providing the **atmosphere** and **opportunities**, however risky, in which strangers are free to become friends, thereby feeling accepted, included, and loved. The relationship thus opens up the possibility for eventual communion among the host, the stranger, and God.
>
> The **stranger** is any person or group not known to the host. The host perceives that this unknown person or group has the potential for relationship as an enemy or as a friend.

Relationships with the strangers in our lives become transformed when we view them through the lens of hospitality. Rather than fearing the stranger as a potential enemy, we focus on the stranger as a potential friend brought into our lives by our loving God. That potential friend may prove to be a source of blessings to our own lives and to the life of the congregation, and we may be called to provide blessings to that friend.

If one views hospitality at the very heart of the Christian faith, then far more than one book would be needed to explore the implications for our own lives and for the life of the church. One book, however, is all we are planning to produce at the moment!

We encourage you to prayerfully consider what has been shared in this book and to involve others with you in study and discussion. While any one of us can practice hospitality, transforming power comes when an entire congregation grasps the vision of what it means to be a welcoming congregation. A separate *Study Guide* is available to accompany this book and can enhance church-wide study.

As you seek to increase the practice of hospitality in your own life and in the life of your congregation, remember the admonition and promise in the Letter to the Hebrews:

> **Do not neglect to show hospitality to strangers, for by doing that some have entertained angels without knowing it [13:2].**

Resources and References

This list includes publications to which reference was made in the book and other resources of which we want you to be aware. Those marked with an asterisk (*) are available through The Andrew Center (1 800 774 3360).

A **Study Guide** to accompany **Widening the Welcome of Your Church** is included at the end of this edition. The guide provides help for those who want to use **Widening the Welcome of Your Church** for small group, Sunday school class, administrative group, or retreat study. The guide includes permission to photocopy for use in your church.

---

*Andrew Center Staff, *Evangelism: Good News or Bad News?* Elgin: The Andrew Center, 1995. Advocates a passion for evangelism and a passion for peace and justice. A very helpful resource for Anabaptist and mainline Protestant congregations having difficulty generating enthusiasm for evangelism.

Barna, George, *User Friendly Churches.* Ventura: Regal Books, 1991. Based on careful research, an excellent look at changing the climate in the church.

Benson, Peter, *The Troubled Journey.* Minneapolis: Search Institute, 1990, 1993. Results of a massive and also comprehensive study of youth in the United States. Filled with useful information on understanding youth culture and identifying areas where the church should consider new programming. Search's resources are all excellent for people working with youth. Write for a catalog: Search Institute, Thresher Square West, Suite 210, 700 South Third Street, Minneapolis, MN 55415.

Campolo, Tony and Gordon Aeschliman, *Fifty Ways You Can Share Your Faith.* Downers Grove: InterVarsity Press, 1992. Extremely practical ways you can reach out with Christ's love in actions as well as words.

A Church for the 21st Century. Indianapolis: Center for Congregational Growth and Vitality (Division of Homeland Ministries, The Christian Church). This outstanding video will help churches of any denomination begin dealing with the changes needed for effective outreach.

*Clapp, Steve and Cindy Hollenberg Snider, *Creating Quality in Ministry.* Elgin: The Andrew Center, 1995. Increasing church vitality through an emphasis on quality – includes chapters on both traditional and contemporary worship. Applies the Deming approach to the life of the local church.

*Clapp, Steve and Kristen Leverton, *Fifty Strategies for Outreach to Teenagers.* Elgin: The Andrew Center, 1996. Creative, practical strategies to reach teenagers who have become inactive in the church or who have never been involved in the church. You'll find ideas here you can put to use right away!

*Clapp, Steve, *Fifty Ways to Reach Young Singles, Couples, and Families.* Elgin: The Andrew Center, 1994. Practical ideas which have been tested in churches around the country. This is an excellent starting place if your church needs to expand its outreach to young adults.

*Clapp, Steve, *Overcoming Barriers to Church Growth.* Elgin: The Andrew Center, 1994. If you can't get people in your church interested in evangelism, get this book! It includes a very helpful section on low self-esteem in individuals, congregations, and denominations as a sometimes overlooked barrier to church growth.

*Clapp, Steve and Sam Detwiler, *Peer Evangelism.* Elgin:

Brethren Press, 1993. Faith–sharing for teenagers. Designed for use in Sunday school classes, youth groups, or retreats.

*Clapp, Steve and Jerry O. Cook, *Reaching Out Through Christian Education.* Elgin: The Andrew Center, 1994. Packed with practical strategies for reaching out through the Sunday school and other Christian education activities. If you aren't viewing Christian education as a significant source of new members, you are missing valuable opportunities!

*Clapp, Steve and Sam Detwiler, *Sharing Living Water.* Elgin: The Andrew Center, 1996. This book is an excellent companion to the one you are holding in your hands! While most church members readily agree that they should share their faith with others and invite them to church, many are not comfortable doing so. This practical, easy-to-understand book helps people identify the natural connecting points which give opportunities to share their faith or invite others to church without being manipulative or feeling awkward. The book discusses both verbal and nonverbal ways to share one's faith.

Delatte, Paul, *Commentary on the Rule of St. Benedict.* London: Burns and Oates, 1921. A classic work for those interested in this order and the practice of hospitality.

Easum, William M., *Sacred Cows Make Gourmet Burgers.* Nashville: Abingdon, 1995. Fasten your seat belts, because this book will turn your thinking about the church upside down – and it will disturb you because Easum is right!

Emerging Trends. A publication of the Princeton Religion Research Center (47 Hulfish Street, Suite 215, P.O. Box 389, Princeton, New Jersey 08542). Has excellent reports on the relationship between religious faith and secular culture. Subscriptions are somewhat expensive, but this newsletter has information you won't find elsewhere.

Gibble, Kenneth L., "Diversity: A Gift Sometimes Difficult to Receive," *The Messenger*, Vol. 144, No. 10, November, 1995, pp. 20-21. An exceptionally well written article, especially interesting for Anabaptists.

Hall, Eddy and Gary Morsch, *The Lay Ministry Revolution.* Grand Rapids: Baker, 1995. An outstanding book on empowering lay people for ministry and setting them free to do it.

History of the Church of the Brethren – Eastern Pennsylvania, edited by S.R. Zug, New Era Printing: Lancaster, 1915. A very helpful reference for this book; primarily of interest to those studying Church of the Brethren history.

Kew, Richard and Roger J. White, *New Millennium, New Church.* Boston: Cowley Publications, 1992. (Cowley Publications, 28 Temple Place, Boston, Massachusetts 02111) Especially written from the Episcopal perspective but applicable to most mainline congregations and denominations. Very helpful in understanding the dynamics at work in most mainline churches today.

Kramp, John, *Out of Their Faces and into Their Shoes.* Nashville: Broadman and Holman Publishing, 1995. This is the best contemporary book on faith–sharing we've seen except the one written by Steve Clapp and Sam Detwiler!

Mead, Loren, *Transforming Congregations for the Future.* Bethesda: The Alban Institute, 1994. An insightful book – helping congregations move into the future. Emphasizes spiritual transformation and institutional change.

Meagher, Robert E., "Stranger at the Gate," in *Parabola 2*, No. 4 (1977), pp. 10-15. This was very helpful in preparation of this book; will be of interest primarily to those seeking more historical background and perspective.

Miller, Donald L., "Brethren and Church Growth," in *Brethren Life and Thought*, Winter, 1980. This is the original essay that got the Oakland Church and Fred Bernhard excited about hospitality! Miller is an excellent scholar and communicator.

Miller, Herb, *Connecting with God* Nashville: Abingdon, 1994. This is a wonderful book on nurturing the spiritual life of the congregation. You should have a copy.

Miller, Keith, *A Hunger for Healing*. San Francisco: HarperSanFrancisco, 1991. This ground-breaking book shows how the 12-step model relates to the classic spiritual disciplines and can be used to deepen the spiritual life. This book also communicates a great deal about authentic hospitality and caring.

*Mundey, Paul, *Change and the Established Congregation*. Elgin: Andrew Center Resources, 1994. An excellent book, based on original research and practical in application. Very helpful in understanding the dynamics at work in your church.

Net Results. (Cokesbury Subscription Services, 201 Eighth Ave., S, Nashville, TN 37202) A monthly publication edited by Herb Miller and published in cooperation with the evangelism departments of several major denominations. New ideas for evangelism, church vitality, and leadership in each issue. A subscription to this is one of the best investments you or your congregation can make.

Peck, M. Scott, *Further Along the Road Less Traveled*. New York: Simon and Schuster, 1993. A book that has changed lives! Very helpful in understanding ourselves and others.

Peck, M. Scott and Marilyn Von Walder, *Gifts for the Journey*. San Francisco: HarperSanFrancisco, 1985, 1995. Many people seem unaware of this beautiful book on the Christian faith. Also available with an audio tape.

Posterski, Donald C., *Reinventing Evangelism.* Downers Grove: InterVarsity Press, 1989. A thought-provoking book which truly speaks to both the Canadian and the U.S. church.

Schaller, Lyle E., *Innovations in Ministry.* Nashville: Abingdon, 1994. An outstanding look at emerging models for ministry.

Schaller, Lyle E., *Strategies for Change.* Nashville: Abingdon, 1993. If your church is struggling with change *or* if it needs to be struggling with change, this book will help!

Worship Visitor Evangelism, edited by Herb Miller. Reprints from **Net Results** articles which share ways to welcome visitors and can be used to train ushers, greeters, and callers. Order from Net Results, 5001 Avenue N, Lubbock, Texas 79412-2993

About *The Andrew Center*

The mission of The Andrew Center is to multiply the number of persons turning to Jesus Christ by multiplying the number of leaders and congregations spiritually alive and evangelistically effective.

The Andrew Center was started with the initiative and financing of the Church of the Brethren, one of the oldest denominations in North America; but the *Center* exists to serve persons of all denominational backgrounds. The following denominations are in a partnership relation with *The Andrew Center:* The Brethren Church (Ashland, Ohio), the General Conference Mennonite Church, and the Mennonite Church. Persons from over twenty different denominational traditions (including Baptists, Disciples of Christ, Episcopalians, Lutherans, Presbyterians, and United Methodists) work with us.

We seek to enable leaders and congregations by:

- **Resourcing** with tested materials, ideas, and services to meet the needs of the local church.

- **Consulting** in congregational revitalization, faith–sharing and church growth, spiritual gift discovery, and other areas of congregational concern.

- **Training** at locations around the United States and Canada on practical topics such as reaching young families, handling change in the church, and sharing the faith with others.

- **Networking** people together for mutual support and idea exchange.

Many congregations elect to partner with us by becoming members of the *Center*. Membership provides special benefits to the leaders or congregation joining and also furthers the *Center*'s research and development. For more information, call or write: **The Andrew Center, 1451 Dundee Avenue, Elgin, Illinois 60120; phone 1-800-774-3360.**

The authors of this book can be contacted through: **Christian Community, 6404 S. Calhoun Street, Fort Wayne, Indiana 46807; phone 1-219-744-6510.**

Study Guide:

Widening the *Welcome* of *Your Church*

By Steve Clapp

This was previously a separate publication but is included in this printing as a service to individuals and congregations.

Suggestions for Using This Study Guide

1. This study is suggested for use in adult Sunday School classes, Bible study groups, church boards, church committees, mission groups, or staff groups focusing on the improving the hospitality of the congregation. This *Guide* may also be used for individual study, but most suggestions are group-oriented.

2. Some sessions may offer more activities than time permits. Extra suggestions may be carried over to the next session, or you may choose those most suitable for your group's interests, needs, and size.

3. The *Guide* is designed for as many as thirteen sessions but may be used for smaller numbers of sessions. Choose the combination of topics most beneficial to your group, but be sure to include sessions 1, 2, 3, and 6 in any study. In some instances, you may want to scan the intervening material and share a short summary of it where needed to maintain continuity.

4. Remember that every group has both active and passive learners. Try to involve participants in a variety of ways, remaining sensitive to personalities and preferences. Encourage, but do not force, participation. Allow "I pass" as an acceptable response.

5. Having class members use different translations of the Bible will enrich your discussions and give new perspective.

6. Your leadership will be easier if you read the designated chapter in *Widening the Welcome of Your Church* and the accompanying session outline in this *Guide* before the time of the class or group meeting. You will need to photocopy a page from this *Guide* for several sessions. There are also some sessions for which you may want to photocopy one or more pages from the book *Widening the Welcome of Your Church* so that group members do not have to write in their books. The session plans assume that you will photocopy the indicated materials and that a chalkboard or some newsprint is available each week. Other needed preparation will either be indicated near the start of the session plan or will be listed under "Optional Preparation."

Session One:
Hospitality: Not Optional and Not Safe

***Widening the Welcome of Your Church* Reference:** This is an initial session, so it is possible that group participants may not yet have received copies of the book. This session focuses on the first chapter, *Hospitality: Not Optional and Not Safe* (pages 9-18), in such a way that group members do not have to have read it in advance.

Biblical Focus: Romans 15:7-13 (on welcoming one another and recognizing that the Gospel is for all people)

Optional Preparation: Put together a short video clip of news stories about threats to personal safety such as burglaries, car jackings, and pick-pockets; simply recording a few minutes of the evening news is generally sufficient, though some may prefer to develop a more sophisticated selection from several television programs. OR – Have available a selection of recent newspapers and news magazines which group members can search for headlines.

Opening:
1. Focus the group's attention on the fears that we experience in today's society. Use one of these approaches, depending on the optional preparation which has been done:
   - Show a short video clip of various threats to personal safety.
   - Have group members turn through newspapers and news magazines to identify headlines about things which cause us fear and anxiety, such as burglaries, murders, drug deals, fires, and accidents from drunken drivers.
   - Have group members brainstorm various threats to personal safety which we experience today. Write those on a chalkboard or some newsprint.

2. Then ask:
   - How do such threats to safety affect our attitudes toward strangers?
   - Do you feel as though you are personally accustomed to immediately welcoming people you do not know, or are you more likely to wait and see how people seem to respond to you? Why?

Looking into the Scripture:
3. Read or have a volunteer read **Romans 15:7-13**. Point out that the ministry of Jesus to the Jewish people confirmed

Study Guide – Page 3

what the patriarchs had been promised, but the salvation Jesus offers is for the Gentiles as well. Paul makes the openness to Gentiles clear by quoting Psalm 18:49, Deuteronomy 32:43, Psalm 117:1, and Isaiah 11:10. Discuss:

- Does Jesus put any restrictions on the welcome which we are asked to give in Romans 15:7? Why, or why not?
- What does the fact that Jesus speaks so much about the message being for Gentiles as well as Jews say about the openness we should have in our congregations toward those who are "outsiders?"

Looking into *Widening the Welcome of Your Church*:

4. Summarize or read the childhood experiences of Fred or of Steve (pages 10-12). Invite group members to share some of their childhood experiences with strangers. Discuss: In what ways is life different today than when you were a child as far as welcoming strangers is concerned? In what ways does it remain the same? What price do we pay when we live in constant fear of strangers? In what ways does news coverage sometimes make the world seem more dangerous than it may actually be?

5. Summarize or read the church visiting experiences of Fred or of Steve (pages 13-14), OR share a similar experience which you've had. How do you feel about the statement of the authors that: "To have such things happen is an abomination to the Christ we serve"? Why do we sometimes fail to be as welcoming as we should be? Why do many of us need to make a special effort in order to be more welcoming?

Closing:

6. Have group members look at the definition of hospitality which appears in the box on page 17. Share some of the background about that statement which is provided on pages 16-18. Be sure to note that there are dangers to hospitality – "And possibly the most distinct and frightening danger of all is that practicing hospitality may change our lives." Close with a time of prayer, seeking God's guidance as a group and as a congregation in learning to widen the welcome of the church to all people.

Challenge: Observe the interactions between members and visitors before and after worship services. How do people in our congregation respond to visitors? How do they respond to us? What initial changes do you see which need to be made?

Session Two:
A Biblical Look at Hospitality

Widening the Welcome of Your Church **Reference:** *A Biblical Look at Hospitality* (pages 19-26). Surprise people with snacks as they enter the room. You might offer cookies and hot chocolate or coffee; a fruit and cheese tray; or a variety of chips and dips. You may wish to recruit one or two volunteers to help provide the snacks, but the activity will work best if most group members do not know there will be refreshments.

Biblical Focus: Genesis 18:1-15 (the hospitality of Abraham and Sarah to three strangers). **Matthew 25:31-46** (on helping "the least of these" being the same as giving service to Christ).

Opening:
1. Have people begin sharing in snacks as they arrive for the session. Then discuss:
- Were you surprised when you found refreshments available? Why, or why not?
- In what ways does sharing food make it easier to share informal conversation with others? How do you feel when another person invites you to eat a meal in his or her home or go out for breakfast, lunch, or dinner?
- Suppose that you were seeking a new church home and visited two congregations. People in the first congregation greeted you warmly enough, but you did not hear anything more from that church during the week. People in the second congregation greeted you warmly, and two different persons asked you to share in meals that day or during the week. Which congregation would feel most welcoming? Why? For what reasons might a person turn down an invitation for a meal but still feel appreciative of that invitation?

Looking into the Scripture:
2. Point out the common components of hospitality as shared on page 20 of *Widening the Welcome of Your Church*. Explain that these components were familiar ones throughout the area we call the Ancient Near East.

3. Have **Genesis 18:1-15** read aloud with persons taking the following roles: narrator, Abraham, Sarah, and the stranger who is identified as the Lord. Discuss:
- How does the Ancient Near East tradition of not even asking initially for the names of guests contrast with our

Study Guide – Page 5

attitude toward strangers today?
- How would such a welcome have felt if you had been traveling in that place and time?
- What would be some comparable ways in which we can show hospitality today?

Looking into *Widening the Welcome of Your Church:*
4. Lift up some of the other information about hospitality in the Scripture which is shared in *A Biblical Look at Hospitality.*

5. Focus on the overview of biblical hospitality which is shared on pages 25-26. You may wish to summarize the seven points on a chalkboard or some newsprint. Discuss:
- What difference does it make that hospitality is not simply a program in our congregation but "the very fabric of the Hebrew and Christian people"?
- Have group members share examples of persons who were once strangers who became good friends or strong positive influences. How does opening ourselves to strangers also open us to the blessings of God?

Closing:
6. Close by summarizing or having read **Matthew 25:31-46**. Ask: How would our lives be transformed if we took this passage seriously? How does it change your view of both neighbor and stranger to think of Christ being truly present in those persons? Share in the Lord's prayer to end the session.

Challenge: Think of one person from your church, your neighborhood, or your workplace whom you barely know. Focus on this person in prayer, and find a way to reach out with hospitality to that person during the week.

Session Three:
The Oakland Experience

Widening the Welcome of Your Church **Reference:** *The Oakland Experience* (pages 27-34). Recruit volunteers in advance for the opening skit, or think about which persons to draft as they enter the room. You'll want to write the starting lines of the skit on notecards for the two participants or photocopy this page for them. Make copies for group members of "Elements of Hospitality in the Church," which follows this session plan.
Biblical Focus: John 13:1-20 (Jesus washing the feet of the disciples).

Opening:
1. Begin with a skit which parodies the kind of approach to evangelism which makes most people feel uncomfortable. The initial lines are given, but the participants may wish to continue or improvise using their own creativity.

Evangelist,
knocking on the door:	I sure hope they're home tonight. This is the third night in a row I've tried.

Victim,
answering the door:	Can I help you?
Evangelist:	I just live a few blocks away and wanted to visit with you for a few minutes.
Victim:	What's this about? My family and I are right in the middle of supper.
Evangelist:	Well, it's about your eternal salvation, so I'd say it's pretty important.
Victim:	We already belong to St. Mark's Church, so I don't think we're interested.
Evangelist:	I didn't know you already belonged to a church. Does that really mean you don't care about salvation?
Victim:	It means my supper is getting cold.
Evangelist:	. . . . .
Victim:	. . . . .

Discuss:
- Why do the words "evangelist" and "victim" seem appropriate for this kind of interaction?
- Why do most of us feel uncomfortable with this kind of interaction? In what ways may that style of evangelism

have negative rather than positive impact?

2. Share some of the background information about the Oakland congregation from pages 27-28. Have group members briefly respond to how they feel about the reservations on evangelism which people in the Oakland had:
- Not feeling comfortable asking people if they are "saved."
- Anxiety about making cold calls like the one in the skit.
- Inability to feel good about oversimplifying the faith.
- The fear of rejection.

Looking into the Scripture:
3. Read aloud or have group members silently read **John 13:1-20**. Discuss:
Why was it difficult for people to accept Jesus washing their feet? What does the action of Christ suggest about the way in which we should approach other persons? Does Christ try to motivate the disciples by fear or by love? Why?

Looking into *Widening the Welcome of Your Church*:
4. Ask group members to identify one or more images of your church which they and/or others may have. For example, is it a country church, a farmers' church, a teachers' church, a white collar church, a blue collar church, an affluent church, a church of social climbers, a bankers' church? How widespread are those images? Are the images seen as primarily positive or negative?

5. Share copies of "Elements of Hospitality in the Church." Note that the words in italics refer to the experiences of the Oakland congregation. The question which follows each Oakland statement is one to answer for your congregation. Have people work in groups of three to five to go through the list. Talk about the questions, and check those items which appear to be areas where your church needs to do more work. Have the smaller groups report back to the total group.

Closing:
6. Go around the group, inviting each person to share thanks for one aspect of the life of your congregation. Then join together in a closing prayer.

Challenge: Visit in person or by phone with two other members of the church this week, ideally persons who are not in your study group. Ask them to share with you some of the things they appreciate about your congregation. Write those and your own appreciative thoughts on a sheet of paper which you can post in your home where you will see it often.

Elements of Hospitality in the Church

The words in italics refer to the experiences of the Oakland congregation. The question which follows each Oakland statement is one to answer for your congregation.

___ *We have emphasized that we are practicing biblical hospitality, and the Bible has been the starting place for our self-understanding and study.* Are our members clear that welcoming people is at the core of a biblical faith and not just a pragmatic strategy for church growth?

___ *We've taken training seriously. We offer classes or groups to train new people in the practice of hospitality.* Have we done enough to train members in how to be genuinely welcoming?

___ *We give people assignments to practice different aspects of hospitality.* Have we helped people move beyond theory to practice in our efforts at hospitality and growth?

___ *We began at a relatively early stage in our emphasis on hospitality to see signs of the concept affecting congregational life. We began to see people lingering more after services.* Do we see signs that our members care about visitors and truly want them to feel welcome?

___ *We had people prepared to invite visitors to their homes for lunch.* Are several of our active members prepared to take visitors home or to a restaurant for lunch?

___ *We cultivated the art of listening as a part of the practice of hospitality.* Do we really care about the needs of visitors and want to help them become integrated into the church?

___ *Classes and groups in the church began systematic strategies to reach out to those who had become inactive and to those who were potential members.* Do our classes and groups do anything to reach out to people who have stopped coming or who might start coming?

___ *In all areas of congregational life, we saw people interacting with one another in more accepting and caring ways.* Do our members show the level of care for one another which reflects deep hospitality?

___ *And yes, we certainly did experience numerical growth.* Are we experiencing numerical growth?

Session Four:
What Motivates Us?

Widening the Welcome of Your Church **Reference:** *What Motivates Us* (pages 35-42).
Biblical Focus: Luke 19:1-10 (the hospitality of Zacchaeus the tax collector to Jesus).
Optional Preparation: Have recent visitors to your church meet with your group to share their impressions.

Opening:
1. If possible, have recent visitors to your congregation meet with your group to share some of their impressions about your church and about how they have been welcomed thus far.

OR – Ask group members to brainstorm two lists, and write the responses on a chalkboard or some newsprint. The first list should cover reasons why visitors should feel good about your congregation and want to return. The second list should cover reasons why visitors may not be interested in returning.

Looking into the Scripture:
2. Before reading the Scripture, ask class members to put themselves in the position of Zacchaeus as they listen to the story. Point out that Zacchaeus had been recruited by the Romans to collect taxes from the Jews. When such appointed collectors were able to obtain tax revenue beyond a defined level, they could keep the excess for themselves. Consequently tax collectors were motivated to be harsh in their dealings, and they were despised by almost everyone. Then read or have a volunteer read **Luke 19:1-10.** Discuss:
   *   How did Jesus first find you: up a tree, out on a limb, ...?
   *   Do you think Jesus' words in verses 9-10 stopped the crowd's muttering? Why, or why not? On what basis did Jesus confirm the salvation of Zacchaeus?
   *   How can we, like Jesus, help persons in the position of the outsider?

Looking into *Widening the Welcome of Your Church*:
3. Focus attention on the chart on page 37 about the reasons for which people visit a church the first time. Discuss:
   *   Are you surprised by the fact that the invitation or encouragement of friends plays such a major role? Why, or why not?
   *   Do any of the other percentages surprise you? Why, or why not?

- What changes in attitude would the chart suggest are needed in your congregation?
- What makes us reluctant to personally invite people to church? How can our motivation be improved?

4. Focus attention on the chart on page 38 about the reasons for visitors returning to a church for more visits after the initial one. Discuss:
- Look at the fuller wording of the items on the chart as those appear at the bottom of page 38 and on page 39. Which of those would people be likely to experience in your congregation? Why? Which of those would people be unlikely to experience in your congregation? Why?
- Note the important words near the middle of page 39: "We are not simply talking about a change in program or strategy. We are talking about a fundamental change in attitude toward those outside the church and toward those who come to the church as visitors." What do those words mean for you personally? What do they mean for your congregation?

5. Read aloud the words about a vision of hospitality which appear in the box on page 41. What would it mean for your church to have a vision of hospitality? List items on a chalkboard or some newsprint.

Closing:
6. Close with a prayer for God's guidance in helping a vision of hospitality and the practice of hospitality become real for your entire congregation.

Challenge: Observe a worship service in your church from the perspective of a visitor. Identify at least one aspect of the service which would be potentially confusing to a visitor. Decide on a solution to that problem, and share it with the appropriate person or committee in the church.

Session Five:
Experiencing Hospitality in the Church

Widening the Welcome of Your Church **Reference:**
Experiencing Hospitality in the Church (pages 43-54). Make cards
in advance for the opening activity, describing various visitors.
Make copies for group members of "How do you and the church
respond to. . ." which follows this session plan.
Biblical Focus: Matthew 26:6-13 (Jesus in the home of a
leper).

Opening:
1. Have each of the descriptions which follow on a
notecard, and give that notecard to a person in the group. Then
ask those persons to describe what it is like to visit your church
from the perspective of the identity given on the card. The
identity should be read aloud before the description is given.

Card One: You are a single parent with one young child.
                You have lived in the community for two years
                but have never attended this church before.

Card Two: You are retired, and your spouse died last year.
                You haven't been involved in a congregation for
                many years, but you are feeling a need to deepen
                your faith.

Card Three: You are middle-aged. You actually belonged to
                this church many years ago but dropped out
                because you thought the minister and some
                members were too cold. Now you've decided to
                give the church a try again.

Card Four: You're a teenager visiting on your own. Your
                parents don't belong to any church and think
                you're crazy for coming. You've only been in a
                worship service two or three times when you were
                a young child and have had little contact with
                the church. Things that have happened with
                Friends at school have caused you to want to
                grow closer to God, and you think you need help
                from the church.

Card Five: You're in your early thirties, married, and have
                just moved into the community. You were very
                active in a church of another denomination
                before the move, but this is the closest church to
                your new home.

Card Six: You're in your late thirties, married, and have just
                moved into the community. You've never been
                active in a church since you were in junior high

school. Because you have three children, you've been thinking that you should start attending.

Looking into the Scripture:
2. Have **Matthew 26:6-13** read aloud with persons taking these parts: narrator, Jesus, woman with the ointment, and a disciple questioning what has happened. Discuss:
- The identity of Simon the leper is unknown. Why do you suppose Jesus chose to be in the home of a leper?
- The woman showed great hospitality to Jesus. Why did the disciples react negatively to what she did? What does the response of Jesus say about his own life and death? What does the response of Jesus say concerning the practice of hospitality?

Looking into *Widening the Welcome of Your Church*:
3. Be prepared to summarize the experiences of Madeline, Brad and Ann (plus two daughters and one son), and Eddie as shared in pages 43-45 and 50-53. How would your congregation respond to persons like these? Try listing on a chalkboard or some newsprint the positive responses which would come and the negative responses which might also come. What are the kinds of visitors with which your church does the best job? What kinds of visitors are most likely to feel uncomfortable in your congregation?

4. Focus attention on the definitions of stranger, foreigner, alien, and sojourner which appear on page 48. What are the different needs which those persons would have? How would persons in those categories experience the welcome of our congregation?

5. Have people work in pairs to complete "How do you and the church respond to. . . ." Then invite each pair to share one or two observations with the whole group.

Closing:
6. Pages 53-54 discuss the importance of "Creating Places for People to Belong." Have each person share one change needed in your church to create more places for people to belong, and then close with prayer.

Challenge: Invite two households to have dinner or dessert with you on the same evening: one household which has been part of the church for many years and one which has only recently joined. If having them in your home isn't convenient, then arrange to have dinner or dessert together at a restaurant.

How do you and the church respond to. . .

- The person who is present every week and who has several close friends in the church? (This probably describes most people reading this book!)

- The person who is regular in attendance but whose closest friends are outside of the congregation?

- The person who attends only on an occasional basis and doesn't feel tightly bonded to the congregation?

- The person who has become chronically inactive and rarely attends?

- The visitor who already knows several members?

- The visitor who knows almost no one in the congregation except the person who extended the invitation to come?

- The visitor who has just moved to the area and truly knows no one in the congregation?

Session Six:
Welcoming Strangers

Widening the Welcome of Your Church **Reference:**
Welcoming Strangers (pages 55-64). Paper and pencils for the first activity. Copies of "What We Want When We Are Strangers" (pages 59-64) for each person in the group (so people don't have to write in their books).
Biblical Focus: Hebrews 13:2 (practicing hospitality and entertaining angels without being aware of it).

Opening:
1. Have group members draw floor plans for their present homes or of their childhood homes. A sample appears below. Have people share the plans and talk about their attitudes toward the home in groups of three to five persons.

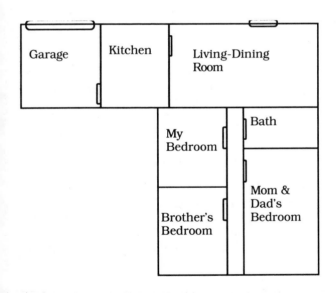

Then summarize the material on attitudes about the home and attitudes toward strangers on pages 56-57. Invite group members to share how their attitudes toward the home have helped shape their attitudes toward strangers.

Looking into the Scripture:
2. Read aloud **Hebrews 13:2**. Discuss:
• If we truly believed this passage of Scripture, how would that change our attitudes toward strangers?

- Read aloud the bold faced statement at the bottom of page 58. How is that statement consistent with Hebrews 13:2? Why are Hebrews 13:2 and the statement on page 58 of importance to churches wanting to practice hospitality?

Looking into *Widening the Welcome of Your Church*:

3. Number off (1, 2, 3 or 1, 2, 3, 4, 5 or. . .) so that approximately one-fifth of your group will have the same number. Have all ones leave the room. Those still in the room should select a topic for a discussion which will begin a minute before the ones return to the room. The others should intentionally try to keep the ones shut out of the discussion, and should not even announce the topic to them. Possible topics:

- Where people would like to go on vacation if money were no object.
- The motion picture which people think was the best one to be released in recent months.
- The television show which people think is the worst one of the season.
- Reasons why the church ought to purchase a new car as a gift for the pastor.

Begin the discussion, bring the ones back into the room, and continue the discussion. Stop the discussion after three to five more minutes. Ask the ones to share how it felt to come into the room in the middle of a discussion. Ask the others whether it felt easy or difficult to shut the others out. What can we learn from this concerning the way that strangers feel when they start coming to classes and groups in our congregations?

4. Pass out copies of "What We Want When We Are Strangers." Have people work in groups of three to five to go through the items, checking those which need more attention by the church and/or by individuals. Invite each small group to share a few observations with the total group.

Closing:

5. Close with a prayer of thanksgiving for the gift of strangers.

Challenge: Go out of your way to extend welcome to a stranger – at church if possible and also in another setting (your neighborhood, at work, in a community meeting, . . .).

Session Seven:
Welcoming Children

Widening the Welcome of Your Church **Reference**: Welcoming Children (pages 65-80). Copies for the group of "Strategies for Greater Hospitality to Children." You'll want volunteers for the skit in step two, and you'll need copies of the skit or photocopies of this page for them.

Biblical Focus: Mark 10:13-16 ("Let the little children come to me").

Optional Preparation: Arrange for one or more children (elementary grades 1, 2, 3, or 4) to be present.

Opening:
  1. Visit with the children who've been invited to come about their view of the church. How welcome do they feel at worship services? At the coffee or fellowship time? In Sunday school? At other church events? How good a job are they doing of helping new students feel welcome?

OR – Share a summary of Jessica's experiences (pages 65-68), and then invite group members to talk about what it would be like for a child to visit your church. You may wish to put responses on a chalkboard or some newsprint.

Looking into the Scripture:
  2. Use a skit to introduce **Mark 10:13-16**. Have volunteers (or draftees if necessary) take the part of characters from biblical times. Let people change the lines if they wish to do so.

Mother:	(Carrying a child) Lord, it would mean a great deal to me if you would bless my child.
Jesus:	(Reaching out and touching the child) May God's gracious love and peace remain with you.
Grandfather:	(Carrying a child) Rabbi, please bless my grandchild.
Disciple:	(Stepping between the grandfather and Jesus) I'm sorry, but you'll have to step back. You're crowding the Lord. Get out of the way.
Grandfather:	I didn't think I was crowding Jesus, and the blessing is so important to myself and the infant's mother.
Disciple:	Don't argue with me. You're just wasting time. We have more important things to do than this.

Study Guide – Page 17

| Jesus: | (Moving between the disciple and the grandfather) Enough. "'Let the little children come to me; do not stop them; for it is to such as these that the kingdom of God belongs.'" |

Then have people read Mark 10:13-16. Ask:
- What does this passage say about the importance of children?
- What is the difference between having a child-like attitude and being childish?
- What do we lose when we no longer have the ability to view life as children?

Looking into *Widening the Welcome of Your Church*:

3. Focus attention on the chart on page 71 of *Widening the Welcome of Your Church*. The chart shows the attitudes toward children reflected in program offerings and strategies in over three hundred Protestant and Anabaptist congregations. Go through the items, utilizing the commentary on pages 70-73 as background, and compare your congregation with those which participated in the study.

4. Give copies of "Strategies for Greater Hospitality to Children" to group members. Have them work in groups of three to five persons to identify the five strategies which would be of greatest help to your congregation in improving its outreach and welcome to children; see pages 73-80 for further background on those strategies Give the small groups opportunity to share results with the total group.

Closing:

5. Close with a prayer thanking God for the gift of children and asking God's help in being more childlike in our worship and faithfulness.

Challenge: Spend some time with children this week. If you don't have any children or if they've grown, find a nephew, niece, grandchild, or neighbor. If you visit with children who are not active in a local church, consider inviting them to share in activities at your congregation and offering to provide transportation.

Strategies for Greater Hospitality to Children

Check the five strategies below which would be of greatest importance to your congregation in improving its hospitality to children:

____ 1. The church needs to evaluate the nursery and child care areas from the perspective of children and their parents.

____ 2. Sunday school classes (or other Christian education settings) should also be evaluated from the standpoint of children and parents.

____ 3. Greeters and ushers need training in how to respond to children.

____ 4. The worship service should also respond to the needs of children.

____ 5. The needs of children should be taken into consideration during any kind of fellowship time.

____ 6. Familiar faces are important to children!

____ 7. Being known by one's own name is important!

____ 8. Discipline problems, when they arise, need to be handled with tact and consideration.

____ 9. With children, as with adults, it's important for a quick response to be made when there is a break in regular attendance.

____ 10. When a church has a day care or nursery school program through the week, opportunities should be sought for the church to show hospitality to those children and their parents.

____ 11. Be sensitive to children with special needs.

____ 12. Be alert for additional program opportunities which can help meet the needs of children.

____ 13. Be sure that your promotional materials and strategies make it clear that children are valued in your congregation!

____ 14. Involve children who are already in your church in helping you evaluate your programs.

____ 15. Provide opportunities for children to interact with older members of the congregation.

Session Eight:
Welcoming Teenagers

Widening the Welcome of Your Church **Reference:** *Welcoming Teenagers* (pages 81-88). Copies for the group of "What It Means To Welcome Youth."

Biblical Focus: 1 Corinthians 13:1-13 (Paul's classic poem about love).

Optional Preparation: Have one or more teenagers come to share with your group. OR – Tape a teenage discussion segment from MTV.

Opening:
1. Visit with teenagers from your church about how welcoming they feel your congregation is to persons their age. How do they feel when they attend worship? How do they feel in Sunday school? How do they feel during fellowship time? How do they feel at events for people of all ages?

OR – Show a videotape of a discussion by teenagers on MTV. Then ask group members to identify factors that would be important for a congregation which truly wanted to welcome young people like those on the videotape.

OR – Ask group members to identify what it would be like for a teenager to visit your church. List observations on a chalkboard or some newsprint.

Looking into the Scripture:
2. Point out to group members that the verses just before the famous words in **1 Corinthians 13:1-13** are concerned with spiritual gifts. The greatest gift is not speaking in tongues or prophecy but love. Have a volunteer read the thirteenth chapter of 1 Corinthians aloud, and then discuss:
   • Why is love so important in the lives of all people? How does loving help connect us to God?
   • Teenagers go through many transitions. What role should love play in those transitions from the point of view of the church?

Looking into *Widening the Welcome of Your Church*:
3. Put two columns on a chalkboard or some newsprint. In the column on the left, list words or phrases which group members share to describe their own teenage years. In the column on the right, list words or phrases which describe teenage life today. Refer to pages 83-86 as appropriate for further background on life for today's teens.

4. Give group members copies of "What It Means To Welcome Youth." Have them divide into groups of three to five persons to go through the strategies or ideas which are listed. Have each small group place a check by the items which need further development in your congregation. Then have each small group briefly share observations with the total group.

Closing:
   5. Close with a prayer of thanksgiving for the gifts that teenagers bring to the church and for guidance in creating an atmosphere which is truly welcoming for teenagers.

Challenge: Spend some time with teenagers this week. If you don't have any teenagers at home, find a nephew, niece, grandchild, or neighbor in the teen years. If you visit with young people who are not active in a local church, consider inviting them to share in activities at your congregation and offering to provide transportation if needed.

What It Means To Welcome Youth

___ Welcoming congregations appreciate the fact that youth are not just the "church of tomorrow" but are in fact part of the church today.

___ Welcoming congregations recognize that it is crucial to provide an accepting atmosphere for teens, regardless of superficial matters such as hairstyle and clothing.

___ Welcoming congregations take very seriously the need to provide a "safe place" for youth.

___ Welcoming congregations offer a balance of opportunities for youth but also recognize that some teens will be more comfortable with one or two kinds of activities than with others.

___ Opportunity to share in worship and to give leadership to congregational services.

___ Opportunity to learn.

___ Opportunity for recreation and social activities.

___ Opportunity for service.

___ Welcoming congregations teach youth about hospitality and how to welcome others.

___ Welcoming congregations appreciate the role food can play for youth just as it does for adults.

___ Welcoming congregations have had considerable success with mentoring programs in which adults are paired with youth.

___ Welcoming congregations have learned the crucial role which small group sharing should play in youth work.

Session Nine:
Welcoming Young Adults

Widening the Welcome of Your Church **Reference:**
Welcoming Young Adults (pages 89-102).   Copies for group
members of "Welcoming Young Adults."
Biblical Focus: 1 John 4:13-21 (classic words about love).
Optional Preparation: Have one or more young adults (18-35
years of age) present to share with your group.

Opening:
1. Visit with young adults from your church about how
welcoming they feel your congregation is to persons their age.
How do they feel when they attend worship? How do they feel in
Sunday school? How do they feel during fellowship time? How
do they feel at events for people of all ages?
OR – Ask group members to identify and list on some
newsprint or a chalkboard:
*   The various life situations of young adults. For example:
    - Single, in college   - Single, in trade school
    - Married, in college   - Married, in trade school
    - Single, working   - Married, working
    - Single, no children   - Divorced with two children
    - ....   - ....
*   What it would be like for young adults to visit your
    congregation. Which categories of young adults are most
    likely to feel good about what happens in your
    congregation?

Looking into the Scripture:
2. Read, or have a volunteer read aloud **1 John 4:13-21**.
Discuss:
*   The biblical selection for the previous session plan on
    teenagers was 1 Corinthians 13:1-13. Why do you think
    passages emphasizing love were chosen for each of these
    topics (teenagers and young adults)?
*   What help do these words offer to churches which are
    experiencing significant conflict between young adults
    and older adults?

Looking into *Widening the Welcome of Your Church*:
3. Go through the perspectives on young adults which are
provided on pages 93-98. As you do so, identify which ones are
true for your congregation.
4. Share copies of "Welcoming Young Adults" with group

members. Have people work in groups of three to five persons to go through the list of recommendations and check those which should be implemented in your congregation. Provide a few minutes for the small groups to share reports with the total group.

5. Summarize or read relevant portions of "Young Adults and Church Structure" from pages 101-102. How is your church doing on the characteristics of structure which have often been identified in growing congregations (page 102)? How many of these are true for your church?

- A structure that emphasizes DOING more than DECIDING.
- A structure with fewer standing committees and more task forces or mission groups appointed as needs arise.
- A greater willingness to trust individuals and groups to make decisions without having several decision-making layers.
- A clearer separation of those decisions which have significant impact on the whole congregation and those which are of relatively minor importance.

Decide on the group to which your results should be reported and do so.

Closing:
6. Close with prayer thanking God for the gift of persons of all ages and seeking guidance for your congregation in becoming a more welcoming place.

Challenge: Share a meal with a young adult single, couple, or family. If you're a young adult, then invite another young adult household to join you. If possible, reach out to someone who is inactive in the congregation or who is unchurched.

Welcoming Young Adults

___ Helping older adults in the church better understand the perspective of young adults both inside and outside of the church.

___ Implement as many of the suggestions as possible from the chapter on *Welcoming Children.*

___ Help members of the congregation be sure that they are just as welcoming to young singles and to couples who do not have children as they are to young couples with children.

___ Make a special effort to help older members understand the unique circumstances of single parents.

___ Recognize the need for variety in worship services.

___ Be prepared to more quickly integrate enthusiastic young adults into the life of the church.

___ If your church is to be sensitive to the needs of young adults on a continuing basis, then you need to have persons of that age range as members of the major decision-making groups in your congregation.

___ Recognize the reality that young adults who have not grown up in the church may not be familiar with many things which the rest of us take for granted.

___ Provide many opportunities for young adults and older adults to interact with one another.

Session Ten:
Hospitality and the Overlooked

Widening the Welcome of Your Church **Reference:** *Hospitality and the Overlooked* (pages 103-112). Volunteers for the drama or skit in step one.
***Biblical* Focus: Luke 14:7-14** (inviting the poor, the crippled, the lame, and the blind to a banquet).

Opening:
1 Begin with a skit about the tendencies of our congregations to reach out only to persons very much like those who are already members. The initial lines are given, but the participants may wish to continue or improvise using their own creativity.

Member #1:	The pastor said this morning that we're supposed to reach more people who are different than we are.
Member #2:	What did he mean by different?
Member #1:	You know, like more of us work as teachers than any other occupational category. We're also almost all white. We simply tend to invite people to church who are just like us.
Member #2:	But suppose you invited someone who was younger than most of our adult members, black, and a resident in another part of town. Who would talk to that person? Wouldn't that person feel so out of place that he or she would want to leave?
Member #1:	Yes, that's probably true; but that's why we need to make changes to become more accepting and open.
Member #2:	But then people will come who aren't just like us.
Member #1:	And what would be wrong with that? . . . .
Member #2:	. . . .

Looking into the Scripture:
2. Read or have a volunteer read **Luke 14:7-14**. Then discuss:
   • Based on this passage, would Jesus support our tendency to only reach persons very much like ourselves?
   • Why is it beneficial to do things for persons who cannot repay us? What is wrong with seeking new members primarily to increase the financial base of the church?
   • What are the rewards of reaching out to persons who are different than we are?

Study Guide – Page 26

Looking into *Widening the Welcome of Your Church*:

3. Share or have a volunteer share the stories of George Miller (who did not sue a person responsible for a stolen oxen but instead reached out to that person) and Jesse M. Burall (who provided hospitality for stolen oxen). Discuss:

- How would our responses today differ from those of a few years ago?
- What can we learn from the way Miller and Burall treated persons who were in trouble?

4. Focus attention on pages 106-108 on differences between persons in the neighborhood immediately around the church and the overall membership of the church. The chart on page 107 may be helpful in understanding this material. In what ways does your church face some of the limitations shared in these pages? How could you more effectively reach out to the neighborhood around the church?

5. Divide into groups of three to five persons. Have each small group look through the list on pages 109-111 and then develop their own list of persons likely to be overlooked by your congregation.

Have each small group report to the total group, and put the results on chalkboard or newsprint. Then decide on a couple of categories for more emphasis in the outreach of your congregation. Discuss:

- How can you more effectively extend the church's welcome to those persons before they start attending? How can you help them feel genuinely welcome when they begin attending?
- Are there categories which your church may not be able to successfully reach? If so, what are they and why?
- Categories are useful in organizing our thoughts and developing strategies. What are the shortcomings of thinking about people in terms of categories? What differences may exist between your response to a given individual and your response to a category of persons? Why?

Closing:

6. Close with a prayer of thanksgiving for the gift of all those persons who are seeking to grow closer to God.

Challenge: Find a person who has been overlooked in terms of outreach by your congregation and get better acquainted with that individual. Seek to involve that person in the life of your church.

Session Eleven:
How Welcoming Are Your Physical Facilities?

Widening the Welcome of Your Church **Reference:** *How Welcoming Are Your Physical Facilities?* (pages 113-122). Copies for group members of "A Checklist on Physical Facilities." Make whatever arrangements are needed so that your class can take a tour of your church's physical facilities. If your group meets on a weekday evening, you may not need to make any arrangements! If you meet on Sunday morning, you may want to let other classes know about the tour so that they will not be perplexed as you go by or upset if you briefly look into the door of a classroom. If a group meets in the sanctuary at the same time as your group, then you may want to ask their permission to walk into the sanctuary for a few minutes.
Biblical **Focus: Luke 2:41-51** (on Jesus in the temple).

Opening:
1. Start the session by taking a tour of the physical facilities of your church. Weather permitting, start the tour from the church's parking lot (or if your church doesn't have a parking lot, from the place where most automobiles park). Encourage group members to view the physical facilities as though they were first-time visitors to the congregation. Encourage people to make notes which can be used for discussion. You'll also find plenty of discussion happening during the tour!

If you are in a very small building, then this activity may take just a few minutes. If you are in a very large building or on a multi-building campus, then you may not have time to see everything. Try not to let this opening activity take more than fifty percent of your meeting time. Be sure to include the sanctuary, one or more children's classrooms, a youth meeting room or area, at least one other adult classroom, the main church kitchen, a lounge or parlor area if you have one, the church office, and at least one restroom.

Looking into the Scripture:
2. Read or have a volunteer read **Luke 2:41-51**. Discuss:
- What, if anything, can we tell from this passage about the physical facilities in which Jesus as a young boy was teaching? Point out that the Old Testament in fact contains many passages giving building specifications to the Hebrew people but that we do not have comparable sections in the New Testament.
- Jesus referred to the temple as "my Father's house" (v.49). If we think of the church as God's house, what implications does that have for our facilities?

- Draw two lines on chalkboard or newsprint and label it like the ones below. Invite group members to quickly come to the front and place their initials at a place on each line which expresses their feelings.

| Church buildings should be functional. | Church buildings should be beautiful as well as functional. |

| As little money as possible should go into church facilities. | The church facilities should be as nice as the church can afford. |

Have people talk about their responses. Obviously this exercise oversimplifies the issues, but it should still be useful in stimulating discussion. Talk about the kinds of choices concerning facilities which your church has had to make.

Looking into *Widening the Welcome of Your Church*:

3. Summarize the material on pages 115-117 on the danger of "Underestimating the Message of the Facilities." Discuss:
- How does it change our view of the facilities if we think of them as a part of the church's welcome? Does thinking about them from that perspective affect where you placed your initials on either of the lines in the exercise above?
- Based on your tour, what are some of the major needs of your church as far as physical facilities are concerned?

4. Have members work in groups of three to five persons to complete the "Checklist on Physical Facilities." Then have the small groups report to the total group, and discuss responses.

Closing:

5. Identify as a total group the areas from your discussion which most need action, and decide how to share that information with the appropriate persons. You may even decide that there is an improvement which you as a group would like to make to the church to make it a more welcoming place.

Close with a prayer of thanksgiving for the facilities which are available for the ministry of your church.

Challenge: Ask a visitor or a relatively new member of the church to share with you his or her views on the physical facilities. How beautiful are they? How practical? How welcoming?

A Checklist on Physical Facilities

Check as many of the following statements as apply to the physical facilities of your congregation:

___ Our sanctuary seats far more people than our average worship attendance.

___ Our sanctuary is 80% or more full at most worship services.

___ Our sanctuary doesn't provide an especially attractive setting for worship.

___ Our sanctuary and other facilities aren't "child friendly."

___ Altar furnishings in our sanctuary cannot be arranged to accommodate drama or other innovations in worship.

___ The speaker system in our sanctuary doesn't work well, and a hearing-impaired person would have problems knowing what is happening.

___ We couldn't add classes or groups without expanding our Christian education facilities.

___ Our Christian education classrooms can't really be described as comfortable and attractive.

___ We do not have a comfortable and attractive area for youth.

___ We do not have all the ramps, elevators, and/or other accommodations needed for persons with physical handicaps and other mobility or energy limitations.

___ We need more parking for our congregation.

___ We have plenty of parking, but it isn't paved. We simply park in a dirt or grass lot adjacent to the church.

___ The narthex area or entrance to the sanctuary is fairly small and doesn't encourage visiting by those who come.

___ Our church office facilities feel crowded and/or aren't especially attractive.

___ It's actually a little difficult to find our church.

Session Twelve:
The Changing Shape of Worship and Program

Widening the Welcome of Your Church **Reference:** *The Changing Shape of Worship and Program* (pages 123-134). Copies for the group of the "Congregational Worship Survey" (which is modified slightly from one in the book *Creating Quality in Ministry* by Steve Clapp and Cindy Hollenberg Snider).
Biblical Focus: Psalm 100 ("Make a joyful noise to the Lord, all the earth").

Opening:
1. Have people complete the "Congregational Worship Survey." Then invite them to go back through the survey as though they had been first time visitors to the last worship service they attended. Have them mark those items where being a visitor could make a difference in response. Talk as a total group about the results.

Looking into the Scripture:
2. Read aloud **Psalm 100**. Discuss:
- Using this Psalm as the basis, what would you say is the purpose of worship?
- We have a tendency to evaluate worship in terms of our personal preferences and in terms of how well it speaks to us as individuals. Is such a view consistent with the perspective of Psalm 100? Why, or why not?

Looking into *Widening the Welcome of Your Church*:
3. Summarize for the group the perspective given on pages 123-128 on "Creating Comfort in Worship." The boldfaced paragraph at the bottom of page 126 and the two points at the top of page 127 merit particular emphasis. Discuss:
- Why does preoccupation with our own needs make it difficult to focus on the needs of visitors?
- What are the rewards of focusing more on the needs of visitors than on our own needs? Does it require greater maturity in the faith or greater security as a person to focus on the needs of others more than on our own needs? Why, or why not?
- The top of page 127 raises two different directions in worship as possibilities for congregations focusing on hospitality. Which of those directions seems most realistic for your congregation? Is there a third direction which would be better for your church?

4. Assign each of the following sections from *The Changing Shape of Worship and Program* to a small group. Ask each group to look at its assigned section, talk about the issues raised, and prepare a summary of the implications of that section for your congregation.

- "A Caution" (pages 128-129)
- "Baptism and Church Membership" (pages 129-130)
- "Prayer and Prayer Rooms" (pages 130-131)
- "Listening as Vital to Hospitality and Program" (pages 131-133)

Have the small groups share their summaries with the total group.

Closing:

5. Focus attention on the "What Next?" section (pages 133-134). Look at the definition of hospitality and the Hebrews verse at the end of the chapter.

If this is your final session, have group members reflect briefly on what they have learned through this study.

If you will be doing Session 13 next week, have group members identify additional areas they would like to discuss.

Close with prayer.

Challenge: Extend a welcome to an unchurched person in your neighborhood, at your place of work, or in another community context; and invite that person to worship with you next week. If each person in your study group does this, there should be many opportunities for you to practice welcoming skills next week!

Congregational Worship Survey

- Are you a (check one)
  __first time visitor? __repeat visitor? __member?
- How would you rate the overall quality of the worship service (check one)?
  __ Poor __ Fair __ Good __ Excellent
- Is the service (check one)
  __ too long? __ too short? __ just right?
- How would you rate the appearance of the sanctuary (check one)?
  __ Poor __ Fair __ Good __ Excellent
  Please write any suggestions for improvement on the reverse side.
- Are instructions for child care, communion, the offering collection, and other elements of the service clear?
  __Yes __No Please list anything which was unclear:
  _____
- Were your physical needs met in regard to:
  temperature?   __Yes __No
  lighting?   __Yes __No
  bulletin?   __Yes __No
  sound?   __Yes __No
  seating?   __Yes __No
- Did you feel welcome?   __Yes __No If not, was there anything in particular which made you feel unwelcome?
  _____
- How would you rate the music?
  __ Poor __ Fair __ Good __ Excellent
  Write on the reverse side any songs of hymns you would like used.
- Did the service flow smoothly? __Yes __No
  Did it seem unified? __Yes __No If not, what didn't fit? _____
- Check the worship variations you would find meaningful:
  __ drama   __ contemporary Christian music
  __ use of video   __ contemporary prayers
- How do you feel about the amount of congregational participation?
  __ The right amount   __ Not enough   __ Too much
- How would you rate the sermon in regard to:
  content?   __ Poor __ Fair __ Good __ Excellent
  delivery?   __ Poor __ Fair __ Good __ Excellent
  length?   __ Too long __ Just right __ Too short
  Write on the reverse side any themes, problems in life, or biblical passages you like to see addressed in the sermon.

Session Thirteen:
What Next?

*This session does not relate to a specific chapter in **Widening the Welcome of Your Church** and will probably not be utilized by some groups. It provides an opportunity to set goals for next steps in widening the welcome of your church.*

1. Share snacks with the group, much as was done for the first session in the study. Talk informally about what people have gained from this study.

2. Have group members look again at the biblical quote found on page 8 of **Widening the Welcome of Your Church** and at the definition of hospitality on page 17. In light of those quotes and the study as a whole, talk together about:

- The next steps which need to be taken by people individually in becoming more welcoming. Invite as many as are willing to share their plans.

- The next steps which your class or group should take. If this has been a short-term group for the purpose of studying this book, then there may not be next steps for the group. If that is the case, think about ways group members can have impact on other groups and organizations in the church.

- The next steps which your congregation as a whole should take. Develop some specific strategies for influencing others.

3. Close with a prayer of thanksgiving for the welcome Christ has extended to all of us!